FOLLOW YOUR
INSPIRATION
AND BECOME
UNIVERSAL

GRACE JOYOUS

The Adventures of Two Best Friends in Search
of Their Life Purpose, What They Discover
along the Way, and Much More

BALBOA.
PRESS

A DIVISION OF HAY HOUSE

Balboa Press books may be ordered through
booksellers or by contacting:

Balboa Press
A Division of Hay House
1663 Liberty Drive
Bloomington, IN 47403
www.balboapress.com
1 (877) 407-4847

Because of the dynamic nature of the Internet, any web
addresses or links contained in this book may have changed
since publication and may no longer be valid. The views
expressed in this work are solely those of the author and do
not necessarily reflect the views of the publisher, and the
publisher hereby disclaims any responsibility for them.

The author of this book does not dispense medical advice or
prescribe the use of any technique as a form of treatment for
physical, emotional, or medical problems without the advice
of a physician, either directly or indirectly. The intent of the
author is only to offer information of a general nature to
help you in your quest for emotional and spiritual well-being.
In the event you use any of the information in this book for
yourself, which is your constitutional right, the author and
the publisher assume no responsibility for your actions.

Print information available on the last page.

ISBN: 978-1-5043-7644-0 (sc)
ISBN: 978-1-5043-7646-4 (e)

Library of Congress Control Number: 2017903647

Balboa Press rev. date: 03/15/2017

Contents

In God's love and direction,
I started this book.

In God's inspiration, I wrote
and concluded the story.

And in God's hand, I release it with faith.

This Book is written based on facts that exist and threaten our humanity. But is not the true story of any specific organization, or person. Any similarity of names, be it an organization, or person is completely accidental.

"Follow Your Inspiration and Become Universal" inspires and empowers the readers to reach for their highest potential in life, and their own true-selves.

Preface

I have been studying and practicing meditation since a very young age, and I have been teaching it for the past ten years.

About six months ago one day, while deep in meditation, I saw a beautiful, iridescent light entering from the top of my head (the crown chakra) and going down to my heart. And from my heart, it spread to every cell of my body and then emanated out to the entire universe. I felt an amazing love and saw the connection and oneness of all beings with God and one another.

At night in my dream, the idea for this book came to me, and I heard the title loud and clear. I tried to ignore it for some time, but the story would come back, haunting me in my dreams almost every night. Finally, I started writing, and to my surprise, after finishing each chapter, the next one would practically download to my mind. I learned that when the universe inspires us with an idea and calls on us to do a task, we show up and do our best every day, no matter how unprepared or terrified we feel.

I have written this book in the hope of shining some light, even if only a flicker of a candlelight, on dire issues facing humanity. I also wish to bring awareness to our connection with each other, God, and the entire universe. We are all like different parts of the one unlimited, infinite source and should care for all that exists. The power and potential of the whole universe lie within each of us. Our task is to rise, break out of the prison of self-imposed limitations, and become as extraordinary as we truly are.

This book is dedicated to those who devote
their time and energy to help others.

Part 1

POSITANO, ITALY

The sound of a late bird flying to catch up with its flock before nightfall brings me back to my miserable reality. I look around in daze, and it takes me a few seconds to realize where I am. I lost track of time and have been sitting on the damp beach right on the edge of the water, staring vacantly at the horizon and off into space. Now the sun has completely set, leaving sporadic, puffy clouds tinted with the beautiful range of red, orange, and purple colors. But I am not in the mood to appreciate these amazing beauties. My mind is completely numb.

I look around, but there is no one to be seen; the beach is empty, and so am I. I wipe away my tears, get up, and, shaking my skirt, climb the steep stairs from Laurito Beach. This secluded, small, and wild beach is Positano's best-kept secret. For decades, it has been the place where locals escape the noise and crowds of the summer rush. And it is exactly for this reason that I came here to be alone. The name *Laurito* derives from the abundance of laurel shrubs that grow wild in this small cove. I am so exhausted that I must practically drag my body up the stairs; going down, it didn't seem this long.

I don't know how long it takes, but finally I get to the hotel and my room. I take a hot shower and drop myself on the bed, letting the tears roll down my cheeks, now sobbing aloud.

It is two days since I have had any real food. For the past couple of days, I have had only water, coffee, and few pieces of apple. I can hear my stomach growling, begging for something tangible to eat. I am starving, but at the same time, I feel sick in my gut and can't eat anything. Even the thought of food makes me want to puke, so I just push my knees into my belly and stay in bed.

I'm not crying anymore; there are no more tears left to release. Now I am just angry, wanting revenge. The events of the last ten days pass in front of my eyes like a movie. Ten days ago, I had a fiancé, a well-paying job in a law firm, and a wedding to anticipate with excitement. I was stressing over every little detail of the wedding, reviewing the dinner menu, the dessert menu, and the decorations. At night, I paced my apartment, sorting out my vows, wanting them to be more emotional and heartwarming than John's vows. That worthless cheater—how naïve of me!

Finally, the day was here. I looked beautiful in my tight, white dress, showing my slim and muscular figure. I am grateful to God for my tons of shiny light-brown hair. I don't care for heavy makeup or big, sticky hair, the kind that, due to lots of products, even a blowing wind can't move. I prefer a more natural look. So I softly gathered my hair back and placed in it an orange flower matching my bridal bouquet. I wore a soft-peach lipstick and was ready.

I heard my uncle knocking. He was waiting at the door to walk me down the aisle because my father was never around. I took one last look in the mirror. I was completely happy, with a big smile on my lips. I walked toward the door and opened it. My uncle and I walked slowly with the music. All the guests were standing, looking at me with admiration. Gliding by, head high, with a big smile on my lips, I heard the compliments, and my entire face shone with joy. What a fool! John was standing with the groomsmen, and the bridesmaids were on the other side, holding their small bouquets. My uncle kissed me on the forehead and went to his seat.

Finally, the moment of the truth was upon me. The priest started the ceremony. I was reviewing my vows silently when suddenly John blurted out, "Sorry! I can't do this. I am in love with Cindy." And with this, he rushed out of the church. Cindy, one of my high school friends and one of the bridesmaids, dropped her bouquet and ran after him.

I was frozen in place, shocked and humiliated, not understanding what had just happened. Swiftly, I was ten again, begging my father not to leave while my mom sobbed and my two brothers stood in the corner of the room, shaking and watching the scene. Hearing my mother's voice, I came back to the present, feeling confused. My mom hugged me tightly and guided me out of the church. And as we were passing through the aisle, I could feel the heaviness of everyones pitiful stare at me. I was trembling uncontrollably. My entire body was numb. My legs were frozen in place, refusing to move forward.

It is embarrassing enough to be left at the altar. Now imagine being from a traditional

Sicilian family and being left at the altar at the age of thirty-two. That was a total disaster and a dishonor for the entire family. My first thought was how to explain this to Grandma Rita—and how disappointed she was going to be. My uncle and mother helped me, or practically pushed me, into the car, and my uncle drove us to the hotel. And since then, I have been crying in bed or by the beach and avoiding the family, not wanting to see anyone, to talk, or to eat anything.

The sad memory of my father leaving us comes back, hunting me in my dreams. As a little girl I was extremely attached to him despite his cold attitude towards his children. At night I cried in bed for months after he left. And now John leaving me for someone else, Why these things happen to me?

There is a knock at the door, and I hear my friend Rachel pleading with me to open the door. I get up reluctantly and let her in. Rachel, my kind and bubbly friend, hugs me, "That is enough. You can't lock yourself in this room forever. Get dressed. We are going out to eat and talk."

The fact is, I'm starving and tired, so I grab the first thing my hand finds in the closet, put it on, and go out with Rachel. We walk out of the hotel and find a cozy, local restaurant. I like to be in a quiet place away from everyone, so we get a table at the corner and sit. I am drained, empty of any feelings, and have a big headache.

Rachel starts with a calm and comforting voice, saying I deserve someone who truly loves and appreciates me. It is better, she says, that I discover now what a jerk John is rather than after the wedding. Rachel is usually cheerful and jokes around. But in tough situations, she is the one who needs comfort and relies on me. Thus, seeing her serious face as she tries to console me, I start to laugh. She says, "I am trying hard to be calm here. Otherwise you know I would be tearing John and Cindy to pieces."

The waiter, a young, good-looking guy, approaches us to get our order. Rachel, wanting to cheer me up, starts flirting with him, but I fall right back into my sadness again, just staring at the table without any reaction. We order our food and two glasses of red wine.

Rachel starts again, reassuring me, "You are strong and will find true love, and all these events will become a distant memory." I appreciate her effort to comfort me but do not see love anywhere in my future now.

I say, "No more men for me ever, Rachel."

She looks at me warmly, "You think that now, but it will change."

The cute waiter brings the food, and we start eating our dinner and drinking our wine. I try not to think about what has happened and let Rachel enjoy her meal. At the hotel, Rachel says my mom is deeply worried and has been trying to contact me, so I should go see her. I call my mom and then go to her room. She starts crying, hugging me, and saying how worried she is; she has been trying to talk to me for the past two days.

I call my brothers to join us. I tell them not to worry and to go back to their lives. I say, "You don't have to stay here. Everything will be okay. Please go back to your work and your lives, and forget about this sad incident. I want to take a few days, and then I'll go back home."

My mom says, "What about Grandma? She is old and frail, and you know how devastated she is going to be. This isn't going to look good with our relatives."

Her insensitive remark makes me so angry that I want to explode.

I look at her with rage. "Mom, please! I can't worry about my Sicilian family's reputation now. Let me deal with that in my own time."

She hugs, and kisses me with tears is her eyes, and accepts to go back home with my brothers.

My family, friends, and all other guests are back to their homes and daily lives. Disappointed, and sad from what they had witnessed at the wedding ceremony, each offering me some words of comfort before leaving.

I need to take some time to grasp what exactly happened. I talk to Rachel, about my decision, and she agrees to stay for few more days.

John and I had chosen April for our wedding because the weather would be pleasant without the crowd of tourists in high season.

Now Rachel and I are grateful for the peace and quiet we can have. She says, "Let's forget about that worthless guy and just have fun." I love Positano and don't want this to ruin my wonderful memories. We like running down the stairs every morning to our favorite café to get cappuccino and breakfast. Rachel has been a superb friend; even when my father left, she and her parents were there for us.

She wants to cheer me up, and I am trying not to disappoint her, but it isn't always easy to keep my spirits up. I loved John, believing we were going to have a life together. Every night in bed, crying, I conclude that something must be wrong with me, How can a father leave his little girl and never look back? Didn't he love me? As a child I didn't know better, and thought maybe it was my fault that my father left us. And now John leaving me at the altar reinforces that idea. I pray, asking God for guidance on what to do now. Where should I go? New York, where those two cheaters live?

Every corner of Positano reminds me of John, and the last time we were here.

Seeing my despair, makes Rachel angry beyond measure. She screams with rage, "That ugly Cindy couldn't find a man for herself, so she had to steal yours. What kind of a friend does that?"

After spending a few more days in Positano, We have to go back home. I hate going back to New York, and even the thought of it stresses me to my bones. But for now we have to go back to our jobs and our families. On our last day we walk to the beach, and go to a restaurant for lunch. And sitting there reminds me of the events of our previous trip to Positano.

Since very young age, I was curious about the world, and dreamed of traveling to different countries. I wanted to explore the world, meet people and learn about their culture.

After finishing law school and passing the bar exam, I immediately started working for a big law firm to aid my mom, so she could teach fewer classes, and have some free time to herself. She had worked hard for years to raise her three children without our father, and to pay for our education. I thought now it was our responsibility to help her. Therefore I put the world travel dreams on hold.

I was approaching thirty, and my mom was on my case to get married, saying it was going to be late for having children. Most of my friends from high school and college were already married and with one or more children. I was in no rush to get married, but my mom and my brothers wouldn't leave me alone. They kept pressuring me to find a man and get married. My mom said she wanted grandkids, and my brothers wanted nieces and nephews. My response was, "Tell your sons to get married and give you grandchildren."

I was happy with my life but felt that something was missing, and for me it sure wasn't a husband. I always thought, *What is the purpose of living*? There is definitely more to life than our everyday routines. I believe we human beings have extraordinary potential and should try to reach for our highest capacity.

Sometimes I revisited my childhood dreams and planned for traveling to different countries.

I talked to Rachel about taking a vacation together, and after calculating our budget, we decided to take a trip to Italy. We had dreamed about traveling there for years, and had been saving and planning with anticipation. We had been looking at travel books about different cities, searching online, and talking to our friends about it. On weekends we sat at our favorite coffeeshop for hours, fantasizing our adventures in Italy.

Finally, we purchased our tickets, got on the airplane, and arrived in Rome. I didn't contact my cousins who live in Rome to avoid family obligations.

Rachel and I wanted to visit the famous Trevi Fountain that is featured in many romantic movies.

Trevi Fountain, the largest Fountain in Rome is a Baroque master peace and a site that all tourists visit. The tradition is that we stand next to the fountain with our back to it, and throw three coins over our shoulder in the water. The first one is for returning to Rome soon, the second is to bring love, and the third one is for marriage. On our first day in Rome, Rachel and I walked from our hotel to the fountain. We passed a narrow alley, and then the crowd of people around this large fountain with huge statues appeared in front us. Rachel and I each took three coins out of our wallet, pushed our way through the waves of tourists, and got to the fountain. We threw our coins one after another over our shoulder and found our way out of there. In the street Rachel said, "Did you ask for love?"

"Maybe, and you?"

She responded, Maybe, with a loud laughter.

We stayed in Rome for a few more days visited other historic sites and had a fantastic time. Then we visited Florence and went to Marsala, Sicily, visiting my grandma. She was happy to see Rachel and me but disappointed that I wasn't married; instead of coming with my husband, I was traveling with a girl.

For our last stop, we had chosen Positano in Amalfi Coast. One afternoon, as we were passing the hotel lobby to go out, I saw John as he walked toward us, coming from outside. Our eyes met, and we just stood there, staring at each other for few seconds until Rachel pulled my arm and we went out.

She said, "What happened, Tara? Do you know that guy from somewhere, or did he hypnotize you?"

"No. Let's go eat. I am just hungry," I replied.

Coming back from our dinner half drunk and laughing, we saw John sitting in the lobby of the hotel, facing the entrance. He got up and walked toward us, standing right in front of me. Rachel and I, after finishing a bottle of wine with dinner, were in a giggly mood. And seeing this guy's face blocking our way and staring me directly in the eye made us laugh.

But without moving, he said, "I have been thinking about you since this afternoon. May I invite you to dinner, drink, or dessert?"

We consulted each other with our eyes and told him we already had food and drinks, but we could go out for coffee. We sat in a café and ordered espresso with some pastry. John and I talked for hours without noticing the time. He said he was a businessman traveling between Europe and the USA. After a while, I saw Rachel yawn.

We walked back to the hotel, and after saying good night, John asked whether he could spend the following day with us. I wanted to see him again, but this was my vacation with Rachel. I wanted to ask how she felt about it first. Hugging John, I said, "Let's talk about it tomorrow." In our room, Rachel and I stayed up until past midnight, talking about John and deciding whether we should see him again.

She said, "If you want to spend some time with John, it is okay with me."

After that, John and I were inseparable. John was kind and accommodating. He invited us to the best and most expensive restaurants in Positano; Rachel and I had been refraining from entering them due to the steep prices on the menu. He was warm and respectful to Rachel, knowing how important she is to me, and if she was unhappy, I would be too.

In the few last days of our vacation, John and I become closer. We talked about the future since I lived in New York and he lived in San Francisco. Every night Rachel and I stayed up, talking about him; she asked whether we had kissed yet.

"When do you think that happened, Rachel?" I replied. "We are always together, and I prefer it this way."

Finally, when we were leaving Positano, he held me, and we shared a long, delicious kiss.

Back in New York, I talked to John for hours every day, in the morning and at night. I was happy, thinking I had finally found my soul mate. I told my mom about meeting John, bragging about how kind and different he was.

"Are you happy now that I have a boyfriend, Mom?" I asked.

She kissed me saying, "Yes, I am happy, and it was definitely time that you find a boyfriend and get married."

After a few months of missing each other and talking on the phone, one Friday night around nine o'clock, someone knocked at my apartment door. Looking through the peephole, I saw John on the other side, holding a bouquet of pink roses.

I opened the door, looked at him for a few seconds with widened eyes from surprise, and jumped into his arm. We spent an intense, passionate night together. The next morning

I woke up completely happy and made coffee and breakfast for us. We had a heart to heart conversation about our future together.

"This long-distance relationship isn't working for me," John said. "I miss you every minute. I am going to move to New York and work from here."

It was the weekend, so I didn't have to work. I called my mom, and we went to her place and introduced John. She was pleased to meet him and later said he was perfect for me, whatever that meant. I think she would have said that about any guy dating me with the potential of marriage. That night John invited me to one of New York's best restaurants, and after dinner and champagne, he proposed.

At home I first called Rachel and gave her the news—and then I called my mom and brothers. John had one week before going back to organize his affairs for moving to New York. My mom and Rachel worked together and arranged an elegant and fun engagement party for John and I, inviting just close family and friends. I was overjoyed and felt like I was living on high clouds. In a month, John moved to New York and rented an office, but he was staying at my place till we found a bigger apartment. After a year, we chose the date for our wedding and decided to have the reception in Positano, where we had met.

Positano is one of Italy's most charming and romantic vacation spots, and one of the top Amalfi Coast towns to visit. Built vertically on the face of a cliff, it has many stairs. Positano was a fishing village, and later in the 1950s, it became popular with writers and artists. Today it's a fashionable destination for wealthy travelers. I fell in love with Positano when we were there and wanted to have my wedding at the same hotel. We had even talked about buying a villa there. A couple of months before the wedding, I thought it would be fun to take a vacation with our wedding party, the bridesmaids and groomsmen. Our friends loved the idea, and we all took a one-week vacation in Palm Beach together. Later, I find out it was during the same trip that John and Cindy became close and slept together. Besides my best friend, Rachel, Cindy was in fact the only single one among them.

After the trip, John and Cindy kept their affair, meeting in private, but playing normal in front of us. What hurts me the most and makes Rachel furious is that they lied to all of us till the last minute. Even at the rehearsal dinner, they acted as two friends. Why didn't John tell me after the Palm Beach trip? They could have just said something right then. At least John should have talked to me in New York, saying he was in love with Cindy, and canceled the wedding. He could have avoided putting me through that painful ordeal and embarrassment, saving the guests money and time. But those cowards had to keep deceiving us all till the last minute. Why? What good did that do?

Rachel is also an attorney, working in a different law firm than I. We have been best friends from kindergarten and then elementary school, growing up together and going to the same college and law school. Rachel and I both focused on humanitarian law and domestic violence. After law school, we found jobs in two different law firms but dreamed of one day soon opening our own firm together.

I am heartbroken and depressed. Every morning I get ready automatically without any feelings. I go to work and in the evening come home without any hope or plans for the future. I take a lot of cases and also some pro bono cases if people need it. I work out, take yoga classes, and on weekends run for hours without feeling anything or realizing the passing of time. I don't want to see John or talk to him on the phone. But Rachel thinks I should confront him, and say whatever is on my mind to have closure; then I can forget that imbecile forever and open a new chapter.

One evening while we are having dinner at a restaurant, Rachel says, "Tomorrow we go to John's office together. You go inside and talk to him, and I will wait outside."

The next morning Rachel comes to my apartment, we go out for coffee, then head to John's office. "If you need me to come and smack him, I am right outside, just a phone call away," she jokes.

I gather all my strength and march to his office without paying attention to his assistant, saying I don't have an appointment, or to all the employees staring at me. But seeing him, I almost lose my courage and want to turn around and run away. Instead, to my own surprise, I stand in front of him, looking directly in his eyes, and let the words pour out. I demand an explanation, calling him a coward cheater, a heartless liar, and much more that I don't remember now.

With a cold expression on his face, John claims he didn't want to hurt me, and the affair just happened.

"How could it just happen?" I ask. "How do you fall out of love with your fiancée and fall in love again with another girl in one week? Did you get lost, go to her bedroom by accident, and jump in bed together?"

But he just shakes his head, and turns his back to me.

At that moment, boiling inside, I really want to call Rachel to come and smack him, or even better, I do it myself and slap him hard. But I pause briefly, catch my breath, and quickly rush out of there, joining Rachel, who is sitting on a bench beside the office building, waiting for me. We take a walk, and I calm myself with a few deep breaths, feeling a little better. I say, "You are right, Rachel. He isn't worth wasting even a second of my time and energy. From this moment on, he is dead to me."

I have been taking meditation classes for the past few months and loving them. Wanting to learn more and go deeper, I enroll in a ten-day mindfulness meditation course, and from the first lesson, I love it. My mundane, routine life goes on: working, exercising, taking yoga classes, and spending some time with my mom and brothers. My fun activities are with Rachel, going out or staying home and watching a movie. On weekends, we go for long runs or do some hiking. Every day I look forward to the meditation session and participate in the class with excitement. I start meditating twice a day in the morning and at night for fifteen minutes, and every day I increase it by two minutes.

I become an advocate of meditation, telling my colleagues at the office about the benefits. I encourage Rachel to take some lessons and make it an everyday habit. First, she brings excuses, but with my persistence, I make her enroll in the class. I start reading and studying different methods of meditation and their effects on our overall mind and body health. But I still feel some void inside and know it's not because of what John did.

Honestly, for some weird reason deep down, I am happy the wedding didn't take place. I loved John, but maybe, wanted to get married just to make my family happy, and my mom would leave me alone. I'm restless at work and feel something is missing in my life. Every day after meditation, I pray, asking about my life purpose. Who I am and what should I do to feel happy and complete?

Almost a year after the disastrous wedding event, on a Tuesday morning, I hear from a coworker that John and Cindy are getting married. I thought that part of my life was over and he was dead to me. But hearing the marriage news is like someone stabbed me in the heart with a sword, and it hurts. Not that

I am in love with him anymore, but it feels like my wounds are still sore from his betrayal.

In the evening, coming back from work, I am totally devastated, thinking, *This cannot go on anymore.* At night, before going to sleep, I kneel by the bed, and as the tears roll down my face, I pray to God. I have a heartfelt plea, saying, "God, I can't continue like this. Please guide me. What is my purpose in life? Please show me the way. What should I do now?"

In the middle of the night, I feel like suddenly the room is filled with light. I see an angel looking at me with kind eyes, saying, "Remember your dreams, follow your heart, travel and connect, and the way will present itself. God is with you."

I wake up, soaked in sweat and trembling. I sit up and turn the light on. Then I go to the kitchen, get a glass of water, and walk back to my bedroom in a daze. The sweet face, the kind eyes, and the warm, soothing but strong voice of the angel were so tangible and vividly imprinted on my mind. I can't say whether it was a dream or whether an angel had, in fact, appeared to me.

The rest of the night I just lie in bed, wide awake, and think about what the angel said, recalling my almost-forgotten dream. I wanted to travel the world, exploring diverse cultures and connecting with people.

In the morning, I get up with a clear mind and renewed energy. After taking my shower and getting ready, I go to the kitchen, make a pot of strong coffee, and call the office, saying that, due to some personal emergency, I am not going to work. And that is the truth, since there is a lot on my mind, and I have to organize my thoughts. Sitting at the breakfast table, sipping my coffee, I start planning and visualizing the trips and adventures. Of course, the first person to share this with is Rachel. I call and invite her for dinner.

In the evening, I make a fresh green salad and a simple chicken dish, and I open a bottle of Chianti that Rachel and I like. At six o'clock she arrives. My joyful attitude surprises her. Seeing my excitement, the set dinner table, and the open bottle of wine, she says, "I am glad to see you so happy, but what is the occasion?"

I show her to the family room and pour some wine for both of us. I sit next to her on the sofa and, raising my glass, say, "Rachel, do you remember our childhood dream of traveling around the world and getting to know different people and their cultures? Well,

I think it is time to act on that dream and want to know if you are ready."

Rachel takes a sip of her wine and laughs. "It was mostly your dream, but you talked about it so enthusiastically that I participated in the daydreaming. Don't get me wrong, of course. I would love to travel around the world with my best friend, but we don't have enough savings for that yet."

I take a sip of my wine. "I know the time is now and hope that you will join me. Tomorrow I will go to the office and give my one-month notice of resignation. We don't have sufficient savings but can travel economically. We have been saving as much as is possible with our income every month; how long do you think it is going to take for us to have enough savings? I say one step at the time. You see, Rachel, we can't wait for our destiny to happen. We have to take a chance and get out of our comfort zone, even if we aren't completely ready. I aspire to find out my life purpose, don't you? We take the first step with faith and go forward wholeheartedly. I am sure that the universe will show us the path."

Rachel looks at me, shocked, her jaw dropping almost to her neck. "I'm glad you're out of the self-pity and complaining mood. But what happened? Did you have a revelation?"

I tell her about the angel apparition and what she said. Rachel takes a sip of her wine and then pours some more. "Please, slow down a little, Tara. You are bombarding me with a lot. I just came back from a long day of arduous work, dealing with many difficult cases. I didn't have time to get lunch and am hungry. Let's get dinner, and we can talk calmly while eating."

"Oh, sorry, I was so excited to tell you everything that I forgot to serve the appetizer." We go to the kitchen and bring the appetizer, salad, and the rest of the food, setting them on the coffee table.

Rachel doesn't want to move from the couch, saying it's more comfortable here. Taking a bite of the tomato basil crostini, she says, "Now go back to the angel. Did you really see one?"

I tell her that the angel was real and that seeing her changed something in me. Then we talk about our travel dreams and how we should plan for them. "Every day here is a drag for me. I need to get out of this town and find the truth about myself, Rachel, but I don't want to force you," I say.

After a short pause, she says, "Give me some time to think about it and look at my finances. I'd love to take some time to do other things. We have to think of our strategy and where to visit first."

The next day I walk into my boss's office, determined, and hand him my notice of resignation. He is completely surprised, saying I can get a raise and in six months will become a partner in the law firm. I thank him but refuse the offer. He even suggests that I take a few months off from work instead of quitting, but my mind is set, and I want a new start. I call Rachel and give her the news. After a few days, Rachel says she is taking a three-months-off, no-pay vacation to accompany me on the trip, but she isn't resigning for now.

I am excited and happy Rachel is going with me. We have one month to get ready and arrange everything for a long journey. Our families aren't pleased with this decision and ask for the reason behind it. My mom says I am ruining my future by leaving the law firm and wants an explanation.

"Rachel and I are grown adults, and we'd like to travel and experience something new. What other justification do you need? I am not going to let anyone influence us. I am heartbroken and need a change. Why can't you understand that? See, Mom, we don't have to follow whatever other people think is the normal way of life and do everything they expect from us. To be happy and have a fulfilled life, we should be true to our own hearts and find our own path, and our unique purpose in this life. This way we can do wonders and shine our lights."

Seeing my frustration, she changes her tone, saying she will always support me in life, and whatever path I choose.

Rachel and I get together a few times a week after work or on weekends to plan our trip, but in reality, it is more to visualize things we'd like to do and all the fun we are going to have. We talk to our other friends who have traveled or now live in foreign countries. I search on the Internet, trying to educate myself and get familiar with the geography and cultures of different places.

As we plan for our trips, I continue taking meditation classes, which I love. They have helped me so much in the past year that I like to encourage more people to learn about the benefits and practice of meditation. I tell Rachel that we should promote meditation and its benefits. I wonder how many people still don't meditate, though there are many studies about the effects of meditation on our overall minds, and bodies health, and well-being.

Rachel says, "That would be a worthy cause for our travels."

As we approach our travel date, we need to decide on our first destination. Rachel asks whether I have a preference. Which country should we visit first? Since childhood I have always had a fascination for mountains. Whenever someone at home or school upset me or something bothered me, the mountains were my refuge. I would close my eyes, take a few deep breaths, and imagine myself sitting on top of a mountain. I'd love to see Mount Kilimanjaro and maybe one day climb it. My suggestion is that we start with Africa, going to Tanzania and Kenya. Rachel, knowing my love for mountains, agrees, saying that she would like to do some climbing too.

We have a childhood friend who has moved to Arusha, Tanzania, and is working with a local women's organization. They bring awareness to domestic violence against women and rape of very young girls. I contact our friend Jane, telling her that Rachel and I are going to visit her in Arusha. Jane is thrilled about the news, insisting that we stay with her and that she has a big place and can accommodate us easily.

I tell Rachel, "See, God is providing so we can take the first step."

Not having the lodging expense helps us a great deal, so we book our flight to Tanzania and start packing. "Where are we going after Tanzania?" Rachel asks.

"You weren't sure about the idea of traveling and now are talking about our next destination," I reply.

It is your fault, Tara, talking so enthusiastically about the journey that I can't continue my habitual life anymore. But we can wait to see how long we are going to stay in Tanzania and then select our next country.

Part 2

TANZANIA

We are, and always have been, ever
pure, free, strong, and loved.

Human beings are like different limbs of
one body, being created from the same
essence, having one source. If one small
limb is in pain the whole body hurts,
not being able to rest. If you have no
empathy for the troubles of others, you
are unworthy of being called a human.

—Saadi, Persian poet

It is a sunny and mild day of late April when
Rachel and I embark on our adventure,

excited but a little sad, saying good-bye to our families. Our plane leaves JFK International Airport in the evening and arrives at Amsterdam early the next morning. Rachel is still in a state of disbelief but at the same time eager about what is ahead. We have a few hours' layover, so we go to a café for breakfast and a cappuccino. I feel so happy and free, wanting to shout and tell everyone.

The flight to Kilimanjaro International Airport is long and tiresome. Rachel and I talk for a while, watch some movies, and eventually get a few hours of sleep. Jane said she has a car and will pick us up from the airport and wouldn't take no for an answer. After we get our luggage and pass through customs, seeing Jane's loving face gives us a warm and welcoming feeling. We do our childhood group hugs since we hadn't seen each other for a few years. Then Jane says, "You must be exhausted and hungry. Let's go home."

Jane has a town house in a clean and safe neighborhood. We enter through a small yard with colorful flowers and some lovely looking jacaranda trees with purple flowers. Jane welcomes us to her, as she calls it, "Humble abode." The decorations are simple, colorful, and in an African style that Rachel and I fall in love with. The house has two bedrooms (each having its own bathroom), a spacious kitchen, and a large living area with a view of the garden. The garden is covered with beautiful red and yellow flowers, and there is a row of jacaranda trees along the walkway.

Jane asks whether we want to go out for dinner, but Rachel and I prefer staying home and eating something simple. Jane has some salad ingredients, bread, and cheese, so we all help in preparing the salad and setting the table in the garden. Jane turns on the lanterns and opens a bottle of red wine.

Tanzania lies below the equator, so the coolest months are during the northern hemisphere's summer. The long, dry season is between May and October. Arusha is located at the foot of Mount Meru in a lush, green countryside and is surrounded by maize and a wheat plantation. It is end of April and the weather is great. Jane tells us, we have chosen the perfect time to visit Tanzania, since the days are dry and pleasant. But the evenings and nights are cooler with some breeze, and sometimes afternoon tropical downpours, since the dry season starts from June.

We sit and reminisce about our high school and college days while drinking wine and enjoying the bread, cheese, and salad as if it is the best meal we ever had. After dinner we chat about our lives and goals for the future, staying up till two o'clock in the morning.

Jane says, "You guys are exhausted, and I have to go to work at eight thirty in the morning, so let's show you to your room." Rachel and I agree, and as we are getting ready for bed, we brainstorm, each throwing out some ideas about where to go and what to do the following day. I suggest that we accompany Jane to her work and ask her where to go after that. Then we can take a walk around the town and get familiar with the neighborhood.

I continue doing my meditation loyally every day; it has helped me plenty, but I still feel heartbroken and sometimes wake up in the middle of the night, crying.

The next day after breakfast, we all go to the women's center where Jane works. She introduces us to her coworkers as her childhood friends who are now two successful humanitarian lawyers. We talk to some of the women about their work, and then after saying good-bye, we promise to go back and visit them while staying in Arusha. I tell Jane we will be back at three o'clock in the afternoon to go home together. Jane gives us a map of town and also some safety tips.

Rachel and I go for a walk, but still being a little scared, we try to stay close to Jane's work. After exploring the area, we choose a restaurant and sit for lunch. We order some foods known to us, avoiding the unfamiliar names. At three thirty, we walk back to the women's center, where Jane is waiting for us to go home together. Rachel says to Jane, "Is it okay if we end up staying here a little longer to explore and take a safari? But we don't want to interfere with your social life."

"Of course," Jane replies. "It will be fun like our college days, and I don't have any secret social life. You can meet my friends, and we can use some help at the women's center if you are willing to volunteer."

We go to a store and buy some ingredients for making dinner. We get some greens for salad and veggies to cook. At home we help prepare the dinner. Jane sautés some chicken she had in the refrigerator. I make the salad, and Rachel sets the table in the little garden. She puts out some candles that create a romantic atmosphere. And as we are sitting, she says, "Neither of us have a man in our life, so let's drink to our friendship and enjoy this wonderful dinner."

We chat for a long time; Jane asks what made us decide to take this trip. She knew of our love for traveling around the world to experience different cultures, but also knows we both are working hard and don't have time or extra money to spend. I tell her about everything that happened with John, along with my broken heart and the long nights of crying. Or maybe it was my crushed ego and damaged self-esteem.

"I was confused about my life, and doubted my self-worth. That is why I had to take this trip: to clear my mind and have a fresh start. Rachel and I talked it over, and the conclusion was to take the trip now rather than waiting. But to tell you the truth, now I am not sure if it was the right move."

Suddenly I burst into tears, saying, "What is wrong with me? First my father and then John. Maybe this trip wasn't a good idea."

Rachel and Jane try to calm me, saying that it's just the beginning of the journey and that it's going to get better. Rachel says, "I didn't get three months' leave without pay for you to give up on our adventure so fast."

Jane says, "It isn't the end of the world, and you will find love again. For now take some time to explore; go sight-seeing and just have fun. Arusha has some beautiful areas to visit, and I can ask one of my friends who has a tour company to arrange a safari trip for you."

I weep quietly in bed till hours past midnight, trying not to wake Rachel. Finally, I fall sleep, waking up in the morning with red, puffy eyes and a totally bad-hair day due to all the tossing and turning.

Rachel hugs me. "You can't control other people, but you can control your reactions and attitude."

"Wow, look who has become a philosopher now," I reply.

Jane gives us the address to the town market and says we can go there and spend a few hours walking and exploring. She says, "You can find the local crafts, jewelries, and variety of little artifacts to purchase for gifts and souvenirs. I will talk to my friend Sam, who owns a tour company, to arrange a safari for you; he will give you different options and places to choose from." Then she adds, "And tonight I want to invite you to a restaurant, where they serve traditional Tanzanian food. The food is delicious, and the owner is also a very close friend of mine."

Rachel and I head out for the town market. We browse for a few hours and purchase some jewelry and little gifts for our family and friends in New York. Before finishing all our shopping, we notice that it is three thirty and time to go back home. Jane has given us a key; thus, we just head home and wait for her. We are starving since none of us had lunch, so we decide to go for an early dinner. The restaurant is cozy, with earth-color tones for decoration.

The owner is a tall, handsome guy name Mark. He is originally from London, England, who after graduating from college came to Tanzania to climb Mount Kilimanjaro; following his climb, he decided to stay for a while. During that time he fell in love with nature and the people of the region, and he chose to move to Arusha. He spent some time learning the local cuisine and opened this restaurant.

Jane introduces Mark to Rachel and me, and tells us how they met in a cooking class. Mark welcomes us warmly. "Any friend of Jane is my friend." He explains a little about the regional food.

Ugali is a popular food made of cornmeal and is served with meat, chicken, fish, or beans. It is boiled and mashed cornmeal, almost the same as Italian polenta. He tells us that ugali is almost always part of the food in Tanzania, as a side dish or as base for meat stew. Rachel and I want to try ugali with grilled chicken. Jane orders Biryani, which is a spicy dish of rice with meat. Mark sits with us for a while, talking about his life in England.

What brought you to Arusha, besides visiting your wonderful friend? He asks.

That is the main reason, and also we wanted to take sometime off work and have some adventure.

You have come to the right place for adventure, and how long are you planning to stay. You are going to love Tanzania, and stay much longer than anticipated. That is what happened to me. Mark mentions.

Arusha is a bustling town, sitting in the foothills of Mount Meru, and is mostly the stopover for climbers or safari lovers; but as Mark says, it has a special charm. We have a pleasant evening, and the food is delicious. I was never a big fan of polenta when my grandma made it, but surprisingly I like ugali, maybe because the name is cute. We thank Mark and walk home.

I ask Jane about Mount Kilimanjaro and the possibility of viewing it from Arusha.

"If you are lucky and the clouds allow, the snow-capped view of this majestic mountain is mesmerizing," Jane explains. "The closest place to view it is Arusha National Park, which is an easy forty-minute drive. I will talk to my friend to arrange a safari for you. But you have to be at the park at dawn or dusk, since that is the best time to see Kilimanjaro peeking out of the clouds. And there are many other attractions."

We ask her to join us; it will be more fun with her.

"I like to be with you two as much as my work permits. You might not come back here anytime soon," Jane says.

"Are you planning to throw us out? Since we love it here, and as Mark predicted, we might surprise you and stay for a long time." I reply.

In a few days, Jane's friend Sam picks us up in the morning for our Arusha National Park adventure. Sam is a charming guy, born and raised in Arusha, so he knows every corner of Tanzania.

The entrance to the park is through a mysterious-looking, shadowy forest. We see the blue monkeys hanging on the trees, eating, and enjoying their food. They don't appear to be interested in people as much as we are in them. One can almost feel the monkeys saying, "Why do these creatures stare at us?

We are just hanging here, minding our own business."

Past the forest lie the grassy hills and Momella Lakes with thousands of charming pink flamingos. I love the giraffes gliding across the hills and the zebras walking peacefully alongside them. The beautiful Mount Meru dominates the scenery of the national park, but we are eager to have a glimpse of Mount Kilimanjaro and keep asking Sam about it.

He says, "It is at dawn, and dusk that the clouds may fade for a short time. For now we can eat at the picnic section of the park while waiting for the sunset and hoping that today will be one of those lucky days."

We walk for a while and keep looking up but just see clouds. Then right as the sun is setting, we look up, and there it is—the glorious, snowcapped head of Kilimanjaro shining under the late afternoon sun. My heart jumps with joy, and I feel a jolt of energy going through my body from head to toe. Rachel is awestruck by the glory of Mount Kilimanjaro, the tallest freestanding mountain in the world.

Sam says, "If we keep our hearts open and receptive, nature can teach us many lessons. My grandfather is a spiritual leader and healer from the Maasai tribe. He says that everything in the world is made of energy and vibrates at different frequency levels. We can communicate with mountains, trees, rivers, or anything else in nature when our energy vibrates at the level of love. By realizing our oneness with God and everything in the world, we silence our minds and open our hearts, then ask questions, and the answers will be given."

At home Rachel and I hug Sam, thanking him for the wonderful day.

I'm not sure what happened, but something has changed in me. Was it seeing the glory of nature or hearing what Sam's grandfather said? The truth is, what Sam's grandfather said about our connection with God and everything in the world resonates with me deeply. But for whatever reason, I feel an expansion in my heart, a healing of past wounds and opening-up. I need to be alone and meditate. Rachel and Jane want to know what is wrong and whether I am thinking about John again.

I reassure them that he is no longer in my mind and heart. I just want to be quiet in our room and to meditate, and then I will join them for dinner.

Jane and Rachel help prepare a delicious salad, open a bottle of wine, and set the table outside. I have an amazing experience in my meditation, feeling completely light and free, but then I come back with Rachel's knock, and hear her saying that dinner is ready. I want to stay in that state, but since it is gone, I get up reluctantly, and join my two best friends. It is the first time Rachel and I have seen the animals in their natural habitat, and she is also amazed by the beauty and allure.

Jane says, "Do you miss John again, Tara? Was meditating an excuse?" Then she continues, "If I were you, I wouldn't waste even a moment of my precious life thinking of that worthless cheater, and you shouldn't either."

"I have completely forgiven him and Cindy, and my heart is healed," I reply.

"I think tomorrow you should come to the center with me and meet some of the women we try to help," Jane says. "They are young women who were forced to get married at as young as seven years old to much older men. And now the husband beats them up every day with the smallest disobedience. We at the center educate these women so they can be independent. We teach them their rights and how to stand up for themselves. We also talk to their husbands, informing them of their spouse's rights, which isn't always helpful, since it is a highly patriarchal society, especially in villages. Some of these women like to go to school, so we provide for that. The others will learn some crafts to work and become autonomous. Then you will see the real misery when you have to fight every minute for your survival, being frightened continuously for yourself and your children."

"I have forgiven John and Cindy, and don't think about them anymore." I reassure you. "But I think going to the center is a great idea, especially if we can be of any help."

Before going to bed, I sit for an hour's meditation and then pray again for direction as to where to go from here and what to do now. In the middle of the night, I feel my angel's hand on my shoulder, saying, "Your path is to help others. Go to the women's center and serve anywhere you can. Trust God, and all will be fine. You are in the divine's hand."

I wake up and call over to Rachel, saying that Jane is right; we should go with her tomorrow and help in any way we can. Rachel is still half asleep and doesn't understand what I am talking about.

"Go back to sleep, Tara, and let me get some sleep. We will talk about it in the morning," she says with annoyance.

But I am excited and insist that we have to talk right now. So she gets up, irritated, and sits on the bed. "Can't you wait till morning? Fine. I am listening."

"I saw my angel tonight, and she said we have to go help at the women's center."

Rachel, falling back in bed, says, "We will do that. Now go back to sleep."

The next morning I tell Jane she was right last night, and we not only go to the women's center but also want to help them too. Jane welcomes our decision.

"Today just meet some of the young women who are in desperate need of help. Meanwhile I will talk to the director of the center to see where you can be more useful." Jane continues, "Tara I think you have been sad, living in self-pity long enough, thinking about why it happened to you. It is time that you get out of yourself, and see other people and the difficulties that they have to deal with every day for their survival."

I say that the national park excursion and seeing the animals, Mount Meru, and most of all the majestic Mount Kilimanjaro did something to my heart. It showed me the vastness of the universe and our connection to everything. I tell Jane about my prayers and what the angel said. Jane says, "It seems that your angel and I had the same idea. Thank her for me."

We get our breakfast and head out for the women's center. Jane's coworkers greet us warmly and welcome our help. The director, who is a kind, gentle woman from the Swahili tribe called Asha, shows us around and explains the order and methods of their work. Then Jane asks me to talk to a woman who was seeking their help.

She is a young mother with two kids: four and six years old. Her face is all bloody, purple, and swollen; she is limping and carrying her four-year-old son and holding the daughter's hand, who is also hurt. Seeing their condition brings back the childhood memory of my father hitting my mom. But I shake that feeling off, saying to myself, *It isn't about you anymore, Tara.*

I take a deep breath and introduce myself to the woman, who is quietly sitting and wiping tears from her daughter's face. The woman starts her story, saying that her name is Pamela. At the age of eleven, she was basically sold to a man who was thirty years older than she. At fourteen she got pregnant, but her husband beat her hard every day, and she lost her child. But later she had two children. She says that the assaults still continue. He also hits the children, especially her daughter, so she has to hide them from her husband. Then she says, "It seems that hitting me and the children gives him some kind of pleasure. He enjoys when I cry and beg him to stop."

I ask her how we can help and what would be the solution. Pamela, who is twenty-five, says she needs help getting divorce, but first she wants to have a job to earn money and be able to support herself and her kids. I want so much to help her but need to talk to the manager of the center first and come up with a solution. I don't know what would be a good advice to give her. I just say, "For the time being, try to stay out of your husband's way and protect your children as much as possible."

Rachel joins me for a break. "I can't believe how these women go on living like this and not giving up." For the few hours we are there, my heart is aching, wanting to do something, anything, within our reach to help them.

"What are we going to do? We have to find a way to help them" I say.

I'm totally determined to assist the women who work there to find the best solutions, no matter what it takes. For the rest of the day, we have some meetings with the staff. Then the manager invites us for tea in her office, saying we can go to the center to help anytime. Jane explains that they have training centers in villages for women and young girls to learn a variety of skills and also get education, learning to read and write. In case any of them wants to continue their studies, they send them to colleges and provide for that. The social workers of the center also talk to the husbands, though they are extremely rigid and controlling. They don't appreciate being told that their ways are wrong. But there are methods, and the volunteers who work at the center do their best to convince these men.

Jane continues, "Yes, it is difficult, requiring hard work and commitment, but it is doable if the willpower is there." We finish the day and go back home. Rachel and I are quiet and deep in our thoughts.

Jane says, "What is happening? You two are awfully silent this evening."

Rachel says, "We spend only one day with these abused, innocent women, and I am drained. How do you do this every day, Jane, and yet keep your energy and spirit up?"

"We each believe that our problems are the most grave in the world, being so caught up in ourselves and our lives that we don't think of other human beings and the great difficulties they have to face," Jane says. "I am fortunate in life and am always grateful for it. Every morning I count all my blessings in life, big or small, and then give thanks for them to God and the universe. That is how I keep my energy and spirit up, Rachel. Because when we focus on all the positive aspects of our lives and appreciate every moment, the universe will present us with more blessings."

I say, "Yes, though I had an abusive father for the first ten years of my life, and my fiancé left me at the altar. But compared to the ordeals these women have to go through every minute of their lives, those seem so trivial now. I was feeling sorry for myself, thinking, *Why did John leave me for another girl, and why did my father leave?* But I am certain now that by helping others, we can heal our wounds and rise above them."

We get home and start preparing dinner. Jane says she is happy to have Rachel and me with her and wants to make a special dinner for us. She sets the table in the little garden and opens her best bottle of wine, which was reserved for a special occasion. I make salad while Rachel and Jane put together some appetizers. We sit in the small garden, and Jane raises her glass of wine. "To you for staying longer, our friendship, and a joyful life of service and inspiration."

I say, "Amen to that, lets enjoy this delicious food and wine." After dinner I ask Jane about the process of getting divorced in Tanzania, and women's rights and if we can help.

Jane says we aren't authorized to practice law in Arusha, but we can review the cases with the center's attorneys and give them helpful suggestions.

"As I said before we first try to improve their marriage by having therapy sessions with the husband, since divorce isn't easy," she says. "But sometimes it is impossible, since the men aren't open to talk about their problems and think they are the best husbands anyway." She adds that if we stay longer, it might be possible to obtain the work permit for us to be officially involved in different cases.

Every day we go with Jane to the women center and aid with whatever they need. I keep thinking, *How can we help more?* I don't believe the center is big enough, nor does it have a sufficient number of employees. I say, "You have to expand, build more educational programs and also a day care to take care of the women's kids when they attend the

Grace Joyous

classes." Jane replies that they lack the funds for that and need more money.

My mind is totally consumed by the idea of empowering women in villages, enabling them to stand up for themselves. I think, *How can we provide the funds for expansion of the women center and its programs?* I remember Sam saying that the best view of Mount Kilimanjaro was from the top of Mount Meru. My heart tells me I have to communicate with Mount Kilimanjaro and ask for advice. Crazy, yes, but what I have learned is to listen to my heart, or it will nag me forever.

After discussing the idea with Rachel, we decide to climb Mount Meru. At first, she is surprised by my sudden urge for climbing but finally agrees, saying it would be an excellent challenge and a perfect addition to our adventures. I ask Jane whether her friend Sam can organize a Mount Meru hike for us. Jane thinks it would be a superb experience, and she is going to call Sam. After a few days, Sam says we have four days to prepare for the climb. Rachel and I have always been active, exercising every day, but we have never done any serious climbing.

She says, "You think we are able to summit?"

52

I say, "Yes, we can and will enjoy it truly." We invite Sam for dinner, and all go to Mark's restaurant. Sam tells us that though Mount Meru is called "Kilimanjaro's Little Sister," it is an impressive freestanding volcano; climbing it requires endurance. People who in comparison with Mount Kilimanjaro don't take the little sister seriously are in for a great surprise.

But Mark says, "Don't let Sam scare you. It isn't that hard."

At night, as we are getting ready for bed, Rachel says, "You really think we can do this?"

"We have learned to say yes to opportunities, so just trust yourself and don't worry. It is going to be fine." I say.

On the day of the climb, Sam picks us up early in the morning. We meet two porters and two armed rangers at Arusha National Park. Rachel asks, "What are the armed rangers for?" Sam explains that because Mount Meru is located in the park, there is a wide range of wildlife living on the lower slopes of the mountain, so two armed rangers have to accompany us.

Rachel has a panicked look. "Wow I already feel better."

We start the climb and go till sunset. The beginning is easy and pleasant; we see elephants, giraffes, buffalo, baboons, and beautiful vegetation and flowers. In the evening we arrive at the first hut and stop for rest and food. We have dinner and spend our first night on the mountain at Mariakamba Hut. In the morning after breakfast, we start ascending to the second hut. This is the steeper part, and with the thinning of air due to elevation, Rachel and I have to slow down.

Sam says, "We can just climb to little Meru peak and go back if you are tired." But we aren't giving up now. We are climbing to the top.

Luckily there are no clouds at night, and we can enjoy the vast, beautiful sky with billions of shining stars and the Milky Way showing the glory of the universe. We have dinner and spend our second night at Saddle Hut. In the middle of the night, just when I am falling into a deep sleep, Sam wakes us up, offering each a cup of tea. He says, "We have to make our attempt for big Meru peak and summit. Hopefully, with the weather cooperating, you can have a colorful, spectacular view of Kilimanjaro."

Rachel and I are exhausted, sleepy, and aching all over; but we are determined. Rachel says, "Every little muscle in my body hurts—some I wasn't even aware of before." So we keep walking and ascending, proceeding to the summit and crossing a rocky path. And then there it comes, the big peak, the summit.

Sam hugs Rachel, and I. Then he says, "You did it. Now enjoy the view since soon we have to start our descent." Magnificent Mount Kilimanjaro's snowy cap is shining in the sunrise. It is looking at us, peeking from the clouds. Rachel and I jump, dance, and shout joyfully, thanking God for being alive and free, for giving us the courage to take on this journey. Then I ask Sam whether we have time to sit for some meditation.

"I remember what your grandfather had said about talking to nature and asking our questions," I say. "I want to meditate and ask my questions from Mount Kilimanjaro."

Sam says, "Fire away. Ask anything your heart desires but wrap it up in forty minutes since soon we have to start our descent."

I sit in silence and start with a few deep breaths, thanking God and the mountain. When in deep meditation, I see Kilimanjaro coming closer and actually feel it opening up and listening. I hear my myself saying, "I would like to be of more help for the women of this region but do not know how. I'd like to reach more women and people in need around the world, people who are desperate with no hope or anywhere to turn for aid." It is like someone else is talking and I am witnessing.

A brief silence passes, and then I hear the mountain talking gently, saying, "You should start a global organization to reach more people. But first you should go back home. Trust God, trust your heart, and the road will light up as you go forward."

I come back from meditation, awestruck. "The mountain really talked to me and answered my question. Sam, your grandfather is a wise man."

He says, "That is great, but we have to get moving. That was more like an hour, but it seemed that you were so far away that I didn't want to call or make loud noises, though Rachel tried some." We kneel and kiss the earth on top of Mount Meru, then follow Sam down. We reach Saddle Hut for breakfast and rest.

We eat a full breakfast, including eggs, porridge, bread, jam, and peanut butter. And there is a choice of coffee, tea, or hot chocolate. Rachel and I eat with a huge appetite, like never before. We enjoy the coffee and hot chocolate. The rest of the day is spent in eating and resting. We lie on the ground, looking at the sky and fluffy clouds dancing with the wind, making a variety of shapes. I always enjoyed looking at sky and watching the clouds. When we were kids, Rachel and I used to lay on the grass in our backyard and find shapes in the clouds.

Rachel says, "We did it, my friend. I guess next will be the big sister, Kilimanjaro herself. But why the mystery? Tell me, what was the mountain's response, or are you making it up and there was no conversation?"

"I will tell you when we are with Jane." I reply.

We talk to Sam and the porters, listening to their stories from the mountains and climbers. We eat lunch and walk some more, taking pictures and then eating dinner. The splendid sunset turns the sky orange and red, and the clouds change color to different shades of purple, as if God is painting them with a giant brush. Then the day gives its place to night, and the stars start twinkling in the sky again.

I think, *How can people see all this graceful beauty and order in the universe and still not believe in God and her presence in all of us?*

We spend the night there, and early morning after breakfast, we start the final descent to the first hut and down to the gate. Rachel and

I thank the porters and the rangers. Then we take a ride with Sam to Arusha. We hug Sam, hoping to see him soon, and I ask if he can make an appointment with his grandfather.

"He is old and doesn't accept visitors anymore," he says, "but I am confident for his favorite grandson it would be possible."

Jane is waiting for us, excited to hear the tale of our climb. We talk a little, leaving the rest for the night at dinner. Rachel and I each take long showers, then jump into bed for a short siesta. Our short siesta turns into a long one, and we get up after sunset. Jane has kindly prepared dinner, set the table, and opened a bottle of red wine. We sit in the little garden for dinner.

Jane pours some wine and, raising her glass, says, "To you for having the courage to take the chance by coming here, and for all your accomplishments."

I say, "We haven't done much yet, but I had a heartfelt conversation with Mount Kilimanjaro and know what to do now."

Jane says, "And did you hear back, too?"

"Remember what Sam said about his grandfather. I am sure you have felt this sometimes."

"Of course, I talk to trees, rocks, and creatures all the time. They are my advisers," Jane says jokingly.

"You can laugh, but I really heard the mountain loud and clear. Or maybe it is our higher-self who shows us the answer in our heart."

Rachel says, "Would you reveal the answer to us, or do you want to keep it a secret?"

"Yes, I was contemplating to myself to be certain that it really happened and wasn't just the figment of my imagination. The mountain said that we should start our own charity organization for helping women and young girls. That way we can reach many more people in different countries. But first we have to go back to New York to start the process, register the organization, and raise some funds."

"It is a great idea. Did the mountain give you a name?" Rachel asks.

"No, I will meditate and see what name comes to me. You two can think about it also."

The next day we wake up around noon. Jane has gone to work. I start the coffee, feeling right at home. Coming out of the shower, Rachel says, "Thank God for hot water, things that we take for granted in everyday life until it is taken away from us. It was really difficult not being able to take a shower."

We go for a walk and do some shopping to cook dinner. I want to make an Italian dish my grandma used to make when we were kids. We buy some salad ingredient: penne pasta, red peppers, a few eggplants, some tomatoes, and ground beef. Rachel makes salad while I mix the ground beef with onion and spices, and make small meatballs. I sauté the eggplant and red pepper with tomatoes. I sauté the little meatballs, then boil the pasta and mix all the ingredients together.

When Jane comes home, the aroma of Italian seasoning is everywhere in the house. Rachel has set the table in the garden and decorated it with flowers and candles. Jane takes a deep breath, inhaling the aroma of the food, and says, "I am so happy and grateful for having my childhood friends here. You can stay as long as you wish and cook delicious meals, not every night, but once in a while would be great. I don't like the mountain for telling you to go back home, but promise to come back soon. But before leaving, I'd like to take you to some of the small villages around Arusha. You can meet the families we help and get a better idea for the future work."

After a couple of days, another friend of Jane Kito, picks us up with a jeep, and the long journey starts. The dirt road is bumpy and narrow. Kito has a calm demeanor, but drives extremely fast, throwing three of us from side to side and hitting our heads on the car. He is quiet, not paying attention to Jane when she asks him to drive slower. Rachel says, "If we survive this drive, I promise God to think less about myself and more about others, trying to be of service!"

We arrive at the first village. Seeing the children looking at us with their big innocent eyes awakens an enormous feeling of empathy in me. Their bones are showing, but they have big bellies, which are the sign of malnutrition. I think to myself, we all come from one source and should care about one another. Why sometimes we lose the sight of what is important in life. We get so entangled in our own problems, that we become blind to much bigger difficulties of others. We selfishly think our worries are unique and more important. But we should realize it is the ego wanting to keep us separate from each other and from our source, which I call God. But you can know it as the universe or whatever you like to call it. When we get out of our egos, and understand we aren't separate, feeling our oneness with all of creation, our spiritual eyes open, and we see the truth.

We stop at the first home on Jane's list to visit. A beautiful woman, about thirty-five years old, greets us, offering tea and cookies. She starts her story, telling us she was sold at the age of nine to a man who was thirty years older. On the night of the marriage, she was frightened and wanted to escape. But her husband grabbed her and raped her by force. They had three boys, whom the guy would beat violently for the smallest excuse. She would try to protect them but wasn't strong enough. One of her boys died in his father's strong hands while he punching him all over.

She had to cook and clean and take care of her children and the old, grumpy mother-in-law. After some years, she gave birth to a girl, who made her husband angrier and crazier; he called the mother weak and worthless. Wiping the tears from her wrinkled face due to much sun exposure and a difficult life, she continues saying that her husband hit her violently every day for more than twenty years, till finally one of their neighbors, who knew of her situation, informed the women's center.

They visited them and talked to her husband. At the beginning, he was offended and upset with the neighbor for reporting him.

He refused to have any conversation about, as he put it, their private life. Obviously when you beat your wife and children to death every day, you don't want to talk about it. But Jane has a magical way of softening people's hearts, making them listen to her. Then she says, "I have been going to the center, learning to read and write, also to do crafts. They have helped with my children's school too. Now I make colorful, big shawls, selling them to tourists in the town's market, earning some money to help my kids. With Jane's efforts, my husband is calmer and regrets his past actions. My children, two boys and one girl, are going to school and are good students. I want them to continue their education to have good jobs. I especially tell my daughter to go as far as she can in her studies. I don't want her to ever have a life similar to mine. I tell my husband not to force our daughter into marring a man without love. And I tell my daughter that she shouldn't get married before finishing her education, and becoming independent."

We say good-bye to her and go back to the jeep. I admire that woman's spirit and hard work of protecting her children; she has had a strenuous life but has kept her hope and goes forward. The driver isn't slowing down, throwing us left and right with each turn. Jane says, "This is how Kito drives. I have gotten used to it; you should do the same."

Arriving at another home, we see an attractive seventeen-year-old girl, who is breastfeeding her baby and singing a melancholic melody. We wait, listening to her beautiful voice.

Rachel says, "I wish she would sing happy songs so that would go to the baby's subconscious. But sadness and hardship are all she has experienced in life." She welcomes us, hugging each warmly. Jane explains that like most girls here, she was married at ten to a man who was much older. And now they already have three kids. The men don't agree to use contraceptives or allow their wives to take pills. Her husband doesn't work; he just makes kids. She makes jewelry and sells them for a little money. Her mother-in-law lives with them but doesn't help her with the kids or housework. The mother-in-law is cruel with her, showing no empathy. When we speak to her, the response is that she has lived the same life and has been subjected to worse. Now she is old with no hope and deserves to be taken care of. She hasn't learned a better way and has no compassion in her heart.

When bad things happen in life, some become softer and build more empathy. But some people's hearts become hard, and they become abusive and angry. I want to know how the center is helping her and if we could do more for her. Jane says, "She is getting education in the learning centers and also learns other crafts. With education she can have better jobs to make more money and eventually become independent. We also continue talking to her husband and mother-in-law, though so far, there is no improvement. But we don't give up easily."

The girl says, "I want no husband. Please help me get divorced. I want to continue school and become a nurse to help the children in my village."

I hug her, saying good-bye and feeling her despair in my heart; I want to help.

Jane says, "The divorce isn't easy here, and besides, what would a young divorced woman with three kids do in this society? This is a dilemma here, but if the family situation doesn't change, then we have to take another approach. As you see, it is a difficult task, but with love and determination, nothing can stand in your way. Because of poverty in these villages, fathers sell their daughters for money or sometimes even a cow. Women take care of most chores in the house and usually get less to eat than the men. The government has been trying to improve the women's rights and conditions, but the old belief system is deeply rooted, and changing it takes effort and big funds for education. As you see, the need is enormous, so any help would be welcome here."

We are ready to go back home, but Kito, the driver, says, "Do you have time for another stop? It is on our way. I would like to introduce you to an amazing lady who has dedicated her life to service."

Rachel and I are emotionally drained and prefer going home. Jane says, "We leave that for another day."

At home Kito apologizes for driving too fast. Rachel, rubbing her head, hugs him, saying, "So you drive a little slower next time?" To that he just shakes his head.

In a few days, Jane tells us that the next day we will visit Susan, the sweet lady Kito was talking about.

"But is he driving?" Rachel asks.

"Yes, I thought you enjoyed the drive, and besides, he is the best driver around here." Jane says laughing.

If he is the best, imagine what the worst would be, so Kito it is.

It is a long, bumpy dirt road, which doesn't help the driving situation. After almost two long hours, we arrive. It is a small house with a garden full of flowers and trees. There is some garden furniture, and a hammock hangs between two trees. Jane goes in first and after a few minutes comes out with a woman who is around ninety years old. She walks straight and agile, which for her age is admirable. She invites us inside with a warm welcome. The decor is simple and modest, but one can feel a loving high energy everywhere. Susan tells us to feel at home, offering tea and homemade cake she made herself. Jane serves the tea and cake.

Susan says, "I love when my young friends come for a visit. Jane has a special place in my heart, and all her friends are welcome here. I guess you like to hear my story."

She starts her life story, saying, "I was a successful lawyer, married to a university professor. We were living in a huge house outside London with our two wonderful, beautiful sons. My husband was a kind, loving man who adored me and our children. I had a fairy-tale life with no worries or concerns. Our boys were growing up healthy and happy. In summers, we would take vacations, going to our lake house with some friends. We wanted our sons to see the world, so every year we would travel to at least two different countries. My older son was in college and wanted to become a doctor; his brother was in his last year of high school. We hadn't been to Africa, so I was planning a safari trip for our twenty-fifth anniversary when that horrible accident happened."

She pauses, wiping the tears from the corners of her eyes. Then with a deep sigh, she continues, "One night we had a big gathering in our house with our wealthy, influential friends. The servers were taking drinks and appetizers to the guests. I went to the dining room to check the dinner table settings, and decorations one last time and then order them to serve dinner. I'll never forget that horrific moment that changed our lives forever. But I should mention here that our lives was changed for a better, more fulfilling, life after all. Our boys had gone out with some friends, celebrating the birthday of another friend. The phone rang, and my husband picked it up. I saw his face go white and rigid. I rushed and seized the phone, trying to hold on to him at the same time. But he collapsed on the floor like a piece of rock. I heard a voice saying that our children had been in a car accident, and it gave me the name of the hospital where they had taken them. Some of the parents were in our house. You can imagine the scene. They all rushed to their cars while driving to the hospital. With the help of some friends, we got my husband to the car and drove to the hospital. I don't recall how we got to the hospital."

"When We got there, we were informed that there were three boys and two girls in the car. Our older son had suffered a head injury and was in coma. Our younger son had a broken leg and some cuts and bruises. The other passengers had a variety of injuries, thankfully no fatality. After some waiting that seemed like a lifetime, the doctor informed us that our son's head injuries were grave, that he was brain dead and would never regain consciousness. But my younger son was awake and we could go see them. We gathered all our courage and entered the room. They both had swollen, purple, and black faces. Michel was unresponsive, lying on the bed, lifeless, looking dead. I kissed his forehead and went to David, my younger son. He was awake, crying for his brother. Seeing Michel like that, half dead, I was devastated but tried to stay strong for David, consoling him. My husband's face had gone completely white, and the corners of his eyes were twitching." Susan takes a sip of her tea, and continues with a deep sigh, "So the long healing process started. David was physically healing but falling into depression by seeing his brother like that. They were each other's best friend and confidant. I stayed at Michel's bedside twenty-four hours every day and would just go home for a shower and go back again. I was grateful that my sons were alive, and I prayed to God for a miracle all day and night to bring Michel back to us. The doctors had no hope and were insisting for our consent to take him off life support. But in my heart, I knew that he would come back to us. I would hold his hand and talk to him, telling him about our safari trip when he felt better and how David was waiting and praying." Susan closes her eyes, like she is seeing all the events of past in her mind. She takes a deep breath and goes on, "My husband and David would come for a visit every evening. We would sit and talk about our future trips and plans. David was well and certain that his brother would come back. One day, holding Michel's hand, I felt that he was squeezing my hand in response. When I told the doctor, he said it must have been a reflex and nothing more. But I had put all my trust in God's hand and would not give up. After almost two months, one night I must have fallen asleep during praying and pleading to God. Suddenly the room became light, and I saw an angel standing by Michel's bed. I felt her hand holding mine and touching Michel's head with the other hand. She said, 'Your prayers have been answered. Michel is healed and well.' Then she left, and the room went dark again."

"I woke up, looking around for the angel. It was almost morning. The nurse came in and turned the light on. I approached my son's bed, holding and kissing him. Then it happened: he opened his eyes, looking at me, perplexed. The doctors came and examined him over and over again. They finally declared that he was well, and it was a miracle. We knew it was a miracle and were grateful to God and angels. I think that our absolute faith and gratitude are the reasons for our miracle. I didn't let my heart become bitter and close; I thanked the universe every day and night that Michel was alive, and had hopes for his future." She pauses for a moment and takes a deep breath.

"Michel came home after another week of tests. At the beginning, he was a little slow. But with physical therapy, yoga, and all the love we gave him, the healing was rapid. He went back to college and continued his education toward becoming a doctor. David was now in college and wanted to study law. I took a meditation course and enjoyed it so much that I started doing it every day. I convinced my sons and husband to take the course. I became more aware and appreciative of all the blessings in life."

"Our twenty-fifth anniversary had passed without celebration. I decided to arrange a safari to Tanzania and Kenya for our son's next holiday. Arriving at Tanzania, we became involved with the region from the very first day. The people are kind and warm, and we loved the nature. We took safaris to see the wildlife. I was happy beyond measure, enjoying every moment with my husband and sons. But I saw the hungry and sick children when visiting some villages, and my heart was breaking."

"One day Michel said that God had saved and blessed him with a new life. So he wanted to help people by coming back here and treating the sick children."

David joking with his brother said, "But first you have to finish your studies and become a doctor, dear brother."

"I know, David, that is the plan" Michel replies.

Vacation was over, and our sons went back to college. My husband and I decided to take another two-week trip here. We would go to villages, talking to men and women, and became friends with some. They told me some tragic stories from women's lives that made me think, reflecting on life and my path. I would pray, thanking God for the miracles in our lives, and asking for guidance. 'I want to contribute in this life,' I said. 'Tell me how. How may I serve in this world?'

"We had a few trips back and forth between Tanzania and London, working for a while and then coming back. We purchased a house in Arusha and every time would stay a little longer. We became friends with some local people and also different nationalities who were here for work or were volunteering in charity organizations. The last time we went back to London, I really missed our life here."

"One night, as I was praying, asking for guidance, I felt the answer coming to my heart that we should move to Arusha, trying to help women and children. Michel had finished his medical school and was in surgical residency, and David was finishing his last year of law school. We had put trust funds and enough assets aside for them. So I spoke to my husband about selling the huge house and buying a small apartment in London and moving here. He was retired and ready to move. When we came back, I did some research, and with the help of my local friends, we started building the women's center in Arusha. It was like that terrifying accident woke me up from a long, deep sleep and turned to my blessing. Earning a lot of money and becoming wealthy is wonderful and the birthright of each human. But I realized that without giving back and being of service in this world, all the wealth, money, and large houses have no meaning." She stops and takes a sip of her cold tea.

Jane says, "Now you know the story behind the women's center and the amazing couple who dedicated their lives to serving others."

I ask about her sons and how they are doing now, and do they come here for a visit?

"They are both married, living in London with their families," she says. "They visit a couple of times a year, and their children love it, and I enjoy spending time with my grandkids. Michel stays longer, volunteering in the hospital in Arusha. My husband and I both worked at the center, teaching English and other subjects. And we were taking trips to these villages for assessing the needs. A few years ago, he passed away. He was ninety-six years old and didn't stop helping and serving till exactly one week before his passing; he had to stay in bed and couldn't walk easily. A few months after his passing, I sold the house in Arusha, bought this small one, and moved here. Women from the neighboring villages walk a long way to come visit me. They tell me about their lives and worries, asking for help. But sometimes they just want to talk and need a compassionate ear to listen and maybe to hear a kind word of empathy and understanding. I still teach English to women, and their children sometimes. We bake cakes together, which is their favorite activity."

I get up and hug her. "You are amazing."

Susan says, "We are all spiritual beings coming to this world pure and from the same source. As we grow up and hear harsh words or go through rough treatments, the ego starts building up layers, trying to keep us separate in the name of protection. Then with the smallest problem, we become bitter and fall into self-pity. I didn't let that happen to me when my son was lying on a hospital bed, unconscious. When the doctors had no hope and wanted to cut the life support, I trusted God, keeping my faith. I never said, 'Why has this happened to me?' I tried to think bigger, to get out of my self-pity and be of service to others."

"When we realize the connection between everything in the world and start supporting each other, with the energy of love and joy, we can heal ourselves, humanity, and our beautiful mother earth."

I tell her about our plan to start a charity and that we would be honored to have her on board. She accepts, saying that with her age, much help might not be possible. Jane says that her wisdom and guidance would be the best help. Rachel and I thank her for the kind hospitality, saying how much we enjoyed our meeting. Susan asks us to stay for lunch, but we stayed long, and she looks tired. We promise to visit her soon and stay for lunch. I hope we will be this active and useful at ninety.

At dinner Jane says she wants to invite some friends for dinner before we go back to New York. We decide on the night, and Jane starts calling her friends. Every day we go to the center and assist in different cases. Three months are almost over, and we haven't even noticed. Rachel says, "You have not mentioned John's name or said a word about missing him for a long time."

I laugh, saying, "Who? I don't know anyone by that name."

Rachel makes me so happy by saying that; she wants to quit her job for now to be able to travel with me. She says we can find jobs in another law firm later if necessary or, even better, start our own. We have to go back to start the process for the charity, visiting our family and other friends.

But first we have a party to plan for, and Rachel and I like to make some appetizers and dessert. Jane says we don't have to trouble ourselves; they are all close friends, and a simple menu would do. She says that her friends come from all around the world to Tanzania, volunteering or working in different organizations. And they often get together casually.

I want to make cannoli for dessert, but Jane says it would be a lot of work. On Friday I bake a fruit tart my mom used to make for weekends and Christmas. Rachel prepares a big salad, and Jane makes some simple dish, as she said. We set the table in the garden. Jane lights the lantern and puts some candles on the dinner table. The food is ready, and she opens a bottle of wine to breathe.

At six o'clock Jane's friends start arriving. Mark, the restaurant owner from England, and Sam arrive together. Then there are a couple from France and other single guys and girls from Australia, Germany, and other countries. It really is an international gathering of young friends. Rachel and I are happy to meet Jane's friends, having interesting conversations with them. We are all drinking wine and enjoying the delicious appetizers, talking about various issues, such as how to eradicate hunger and malnutrition, illiteracy, and human trafficking—and how to save our planet.

Around seven the doorbell rings again, and since Jane is busy, Rachel goes to open the door. She opens the door, and I see her standing motionless, as if a jolt of electricity has gone through her entire body. I take a step toward her to find out what is wrong, and then it becomes clear that everything is perfect. On the other side of the door, in front of her, stands this tall guy with the most exquisite emerald-green eyes and a smile. "Hello. I am Tony, Jane's friend. May I come in?"

Blushing, Rachel shakes his hand, introducing herself and saying, "Yes, of course."

Jane says, "Oh, Tony, I see you already met one of my childhood friends."

Looking at Rachel, he smiles, saying, "But you hadn't told us how beautiful and charming they are." Tony and I shake hands and exchange a few words, and then I go to the kitchen with Jane to help bring the food out.

Jane, raising her wine glass, says, "A salute to my old friends, who are visiting from New

York. But, they have decided to stay longer and maybe join our group."

But I don't think Rachel or Tony heard Jane or anyone else talking. They sit next to each other at the dinner table, talking and laughing like no one else exist. Jane asks me to talk about our plan for starting our charity work in Tanzania and expanding to other countries. The French couple, Gabrielle and her husband, Paul, say they are interested in joining and helping. Paul has a business, and travels between France and Tanzania, and Gabrielle's parents moved here when she was a little girl.

We spend a very pleasant evening, but it is almost two in the morning when the guests start leaving, wishing Rachel and me a safe trip and a speedy return. Saying good-bye to Sam, I ask whether he has made an appointment with his grandfather.

He says, "I asked, but grandpa said it is better when you and Rachel are back from New York."

"How did he know? Did you tell him?" I ask surprised.

"He is aware of everything. I could never hide anything from him, it is scary, Tara." replies Sam

Tony is the last to leave but not willingly since Jane practically pushes him out the door, saying we are tired.

When he finally leaves, Jane says, "What happened, Rachel? Where were you? Did you get lost in those emerald eyes and couldn't find the way back?"

I say, "Jane is right. You ignored all of us the entire night."

Rachel says, "Tony was just telling me about himself and you two are making a big deal out of nothing."

"Tell me about this nothing," I say.

"He is from Liverpool, England. He traveled to Tanzania a few years ago after graduating from college to climb Mount Kilimanjaro. Following the summit, he took a safari, during which he fell in love with nature and the wildlife in this area. He goes back to England packs his stuff and moves here, working with a wildlife preservation group. And then I was talking about our trip home and our charity and my two best friends."

Jane and I laugh, saying, "Okay, Rachel, you are forgiven."

Our departure to the United States is coming up, so we go to the town market to buy some souvenirs for family members and friends back home. At home Jane says that Tony has invited us to dinner.

"And he couldn't stop talking about how wonderful you are, Rachel. All the single girls here were after him with those emerald-green eyes. And here you come, stealing his heart without any effort."

Rachel blushes, and looking at us agitated, says, "I didn't steal anything of him. We just met, and I am not sure about him yet."

With that reaction, I say, "You are in love, Rachel," but we leave it at that.

In the evening, Tony comes and takes us to the most expensive restaurant in town. The food is delicious, and Tony orders the best wine, which we enjoy greatly. He asks Rachel whether she would like to go for a wildlife tour before our trip back home. She hesitates for a moment, but with my kick from under the table, she agrees to go with him.

The next day we go with Jane to say farewell to her coworkers and the young girls in the education center, promising to be back soon. Seeing their sad faces, I feel so connected to these girls and don't want to leave them.

The next day Rachel and Tony go for a wildlife tour, and I go to work with Jane to spend some more time with the girls before we leave. In the evening when Rachel comes back, Jane and I ask about her day and whether Tony kissed her.

Rachel says, "Slow down with the questions. I tell you he was a perfect gentleman. We talked all day like two old friends who have known each other forever." She pauses for few seconds, then continues, "And we kissed at the door, saying good-bye. And just when I meet someone who is likable, we have to leave before having a chance to know him better."

Jane says, "That gives you an incentive to come back even sooner."

On the day of our departure, Tony takes us to the airport. Saying good-bye is always sad, but the thought of a reunion makes it easier. Tony holds Rachel for a long time, whispering something in her ears. On the plane, Rachel cries, saying she might be in love.

I say, "There is no might. You *are* in love, Rachel. See, you opened the door to endless possibilities by saying yes to this opportunity and taking the trip with me. When you take a chance and get out of your comfort zone, the universe opens its door and brings unexpected blessings to you."

She says, "I am sure true love will find you, Tara."

"My focus isn't on myself now, but on finding the ways to be of more service to people in need." I answer.

When we arrive in New York, one of my brothers is waiting for us at the airport. He drives us to my mom's house for a welcome party. Both of our families and close friends are gathering to see and greet us back. The guests have each brought a dish; it is a feast of delicious food and loving company. They bombard us with questions about the trip and all our adventures. But my mom comes to the rescue and says, "There will be time for all the questions. They had a long flight and need to get some rest. We are all grateful to have them back safely."

After the guests leave, Rachel says she doesn't want to separate from me and go to her apartment alone. We have been together every day and at night have chatted in bed for hours. She asks if she can spend the first night at my place. I respond, "Of course. You should stay with me till we go back. It would be easier to work on our projects." My brother drives us to my apartment, helps with our luggage, and leaves. We take long showers and go to bed.

We wake up early in the morning and go out for coffee. Walking to the coffee shop, I look around. People are rushing to wherever is their destination without any smile or even a look at each other. It feels strange to be back with life being so different here; people are more into themselves.

"If you pay closer attention, Rachel, you notice most people are frowning, looking stressed, and hardly smiling." We get to the coffee shop and stand in the long line. I smile, looking at people, but heads are all down, since they are playing with their cell phones. It is the same in elevators; everybody is looking down at his or her shoes or phone, trying to avoid eye contact. Sometimes a kind look and a smile can make a difference in someone's day by changing his or her mood. We get our coffee and sit. I suggest that we make a list of friends we would like to ask for the charity board and then narrow it down. The board can consist of five or seven people who want to be more involved, and can dedicate some time, and meet regularly. They oversee the projects and make decisions. We can invite our friends for drinks and appetizers, telling them about our idea and see who is in and wants to help. Some of our friends might not be interested at all, or help whenever they can.

Rachel says we should take care of things here as soon as possible and go back since Arusha feels like home now. I laugh, saying, "Looking into Tony's green eyes is home for you now."

She says, "Yes, I admit that, but there is more to it. You have influenced me to serve and make a difference in the world. I can't continue my everyday life here like before."

I say, "Yes it would be good to go back as soon as possible, but we have to make some money for our expenses and travels. We also need a name for the charity to register it. I will ask my angel tonight."

At night after my meditation, I pray, asking God to support and guide us in our mission. Then I ask my angel to bring me a name for our organization. I fall into a deep sleep and see my angel shining a white light in my heart, and all around the room, it feels so comfortable and sweet. Then I hear and feel my angel saying, "Reach out, Tara. You should reach as high and as far as you can with an open heart. And touch as many people as possible with your reach." I hear her voice and also see it deep in my heart with a new sensation.

I wake up, running to the guest room and calling for Rachel. "I know the name for our charity. It is Reach."

"Let's sleep. I should be used to these middle-of-the-night messages by now, but can't you wait till morning to tell me?" Rachel turns her back, pulling the blanket up on her head.

In the morning, I make coffee and breakfast for Rachel, saying that next time she will hear the news in the morning—that is, if I can tame my enthusiasm. She hugs me, saying I can call her anytime of the night when my angel appears. We call Jane, asking her about the name, which she likes and approves of. We write the list of our friends' names and start calling, inviting them for the coming Sunday evening event with appetizers and drinks.

Rachel and I tell our friends about the trip, the experiences we had, and people we met who led to this decision. Most of our friends would like to take part as board or advisory board members. Even the ones who refuse due to demanding jobs or family responsibilities promise to help financially and spread the word to bring more funds. I start the legal process of registering the organization and do all the required steps.

We want to have a fund-raising gala. One of our friends, Sara, is an event organizer for Fortune 500 companies and other charities; she agrees to help us. She wants to organize a high-class gala, inviting her influential friends and clients to donate money for the charity. Jane has flown in from Tanzania to participate in our first fund-raising event.

At the night of the gala, the three of us look fantastic; I should say. Sara has outdone herself by organizing a truly amazing gala; decorations is elegant, the white and purple flowers are artfully arranged, food, and everything else are flawless. I give an emotional and passionate speech about the people we met and their heartbreaking and, at the same time inspiring stories. And I share about our encounters with people who have dedicated their lives to serving others. I then talk about the enormous need for help, explaining our mission. The event goes extremely well, exceeding our expectations by raising half a million dollars.

At the end of the event, Sara tells me she wants to join the Reach Charity; this is great news since she has many friends, and can do fund-raising, even when we go back to Tanzania. We stay up till morning talking about the success of the first event. I think when people come together, putting aside their differences, jealousy, and competition with kindness and generosity, they can perform marvels.

Jane stays for two weeks, visiting her family but spending most of the time with Rachel and me. We take a short trip to Washington, DC, visiting some college friends who now live and work there. Before Jane's departure, we arrange a meeting with the members of Reach to discuss the distributions of the funds. We agree to open an educational center for women and young girls in Tanzania and leave the rest of the funds for another country.

Jane is leaving, and we are sad, but we promise her to finish our work and go back soon. Rachel talks to Tony on the phone as often as possible, and they exchange e-mails, but every night before bed, she tells me how much they miss each other. I love Rachel and try to comfort her, but sometimes I really want to say, "It isn't a long time, so stop whining."

We are in New York for almost two months, and everything is set in motion for our organization so Rachel and I can leave with peace of mind. Our families aren't happy with this separation again. I have to reassure my mom that our plan isn't to move to Arusha; we will come back to New York, though now with Tony living there, I'm not certain about Rachel, whether she wants to go back.

We arrive at Kilimanjaro airport in the evening. Tony and Jane are waiting for us outside the passport check. Rachel runs into Tony's arm, kissing him on the lips with no hesitation. At Jane's place, Tony stays, talking to Rachel for a while, and then leaves so we can get some sleep. Jane and I tease Rachel about the long French kiss. Rachel, laughing joyfully, says, "I am in love for the first time in my life and don't want to waste any time."

We sit with Jane, talking for a while, and then go to our room, which has a warm and familiar feeling. The next day Jane asks whether we need a day to recuperate from the long trip. But we are excited to go to the women's center and see her coworkers, who have become our friends, and tell them about our trip.

Jane has already obtained the permission to build an educational center under the name of Reach for women and girls in low-income families. Everything is ready for the start of the building. We want to invite Susan to the event, but Jane says the long, bumpy road would be hard for her. Maybe when the center is ready for the opening, she can join us. But when Susan hears that Rachel and I are back and learns our plan for the education center, she insists in joining us now that she is well and has the energy. Rachel says, "But please send a more gentle driver, since she is old and frail."

Jane says, "Don't worry. That was a fun drive just for you two; for Susan I have another driver."

We all congregate at the site, waiting for Susan. The women who know her and whom she has helped for many years are present. When she arrives, she hugs every one of them, asking about their current life and situation. After the ceremony of starting the building, we go to the women's center for tea, cookies, and Arusha's specialty pear cake, which Susan likes.

Everyone working at the center or somehow knowing Susan loves and enjoys listening to her stories. But she is getting tired and wants to go home. I invite her to spend the night at Jane's, but Susan prefers to go home, saying she has never missed her daily meditation and doesn't want it to happen now. She then says that it gives her energy and clarity, and has been a great help through many hardships in her life.

She looks at me. "You understand that, Tara, and have experienced the benefits of it, so encourage your friends to make meditation a daily habit." We thank her for enduring the long road and joining us.

But she says, "Don't leave the things that you want to do today for the next day, since the next day might not come." She then says, "I want to continue my service, doing the things that are dear to my heart. This way I leave the world with no unfinished business or regrets. When inspirations and ideas come to you, take action courageously, without hesitation or delay, my dear girls, and come visit me soon."

The building of the women's educational center is going well. We have decided the budget for it, and Jane is going to oversee the operation. We are in contact with the board and advisory board members is New York, exchanging ideas for new projects, and Sara has plans for more fund-raising.

Rachel and Tony go out most evenings for a walk or dinner. Jane and I go to Mark's restaurant some evenings, meeting Paul and Gabrielle and talking about our future projects for helping victims of domestic violence and rape. Or we just stay home, chatting; that I enjoy a lot. We talk till Rachel gets home and gives us the scope. I do longer meditation, and go for walks every morning, early before that Rachel and Jane wakeup. I contemplate our next project, and think about other countries in need of help.

One evening when Rachel isn't going out with Tony, we make food. Jane opens a bottle of wine, and the three of us sit for dinner. As we are enjoying our wine, I say, "It is good to have you home, Rachel, even if it is just for tonight. I have been asking for guidance about our next step and feel that it is time to expand our work to more countries."

Rachel says, "Oh no, we just got back, and I can't leave Tony again. Not after he admitted to be madly in love with me."

"I am sharing this with you because my angel told me that we need to expand our work to more countries. But I don't want to force you, Rachel, to do anything against your desire. Remember what Susan said. You should meditate and ask the question yourself. You left your job to continue helping, not staying here for Tony, no matter how irresistible those green eyes are!" She looks at me with such a sad face that I hug her, saying, "That was a joke, and if you prefer to stay in Arusha, it is okay with me."

In our room before going to bed, I sit for a long meditation. Then I pray, asking my angel to bring divine guidance to me about where to go from here. I see my kind angel, who by now is so familiar. She says, "Tara, you are meant to take your Reach high and far. Don't get disappointed now, even if your friend wouldn't want to follow your path. Go to Nepal; you can do plenty of help there. Go with service in mind, and you will not be alone. God is with you, providing all the necessary resources."

In the morning I wake up, energetic and cheerful, saying, "We have to go to Nepal—that is, if you want to join me Rachel."

Jane says, "Why Nepal? It is on top of the mountains and freezing."

"It isn't on top of the mountains and has a milder season so that we can go," I say. "Rachel, you can talk to Tony if you want before deciding."

Rachel says, "I like our work here, and of course Tony is important to me. But don't you ever think I am going to leave my best friend alone. We started the journey together and will continue it together. This is my mission too."

Then she says, "Tony isn't going to be happy about it, but I will make him understand."

I share what my angel said about taking our Reach high and far with Rachel and Jane. Rachel, laughing, says, "It is your angel who is causing all these troubles but thanks for waiting till morning to tell us this time."

"What are you complaining about?" I say. "You are doing a good deed helping others and found the love of your life. If you hadn't taken the chance, would there be any Tony now?"

She says, "Just joking, I love your angel for guiding us, but I don't want to break Tony's heart."

"We aren't staying in Nepal forever. Talk to him and see what he says."

I ask Jane whether she or any of her friends know anyone volunteering in Nepal for women's organizations. I also do some research about the international organizations working to improve women's lives in Nepal. Mark tells us that one of his childhood friends from England, Jack, is in Katmandu and working with a group against human trafficking. He is from a wealthy family and has the kindest heart ever. His passion is to help wherever he can and for now is volunteering in Nepal. This is much-appreciated news to Rachel and me, and I say that it helps knowing someone is there to assist us if we need. Mark is going to contact his friend in Kathmandu to tell him we are traveling to Nepal and asking for his help.

Rachel invites Tony for a romantic dinner, saying she wants to treat him this time and to break the news of going to Nepal. Tony picks her up from Jane's house, and they go to a cozy local restaurant, where she had made reservation. I wish her luck, saying, "Come back with his approval."

"While sipping our wine, waiting for the food, I cautiously brought the conversation to the Nepal's trip, saying we want to expand our help," Rachel tells us later. "Tony was surprised, upset, and angry, saying, 'I just came back,' and he can't lose me again. All my kisses and explanations that we will be back soon weren't working. Tony is in love and wants to be with me. Then he said if I have to travel to Nepal, so be it; he is going with us too. I loved the idea but said, 'What about your work here?' Tony said he had come here to volunteer for one year but stayed longer for me and can leave anytime with a short notice. His plan was to go back after a year and pursue his education, obtaining a PhD in psychology. Now he is going to travel to Nepal and after that to wherever else I go. Then Tony said that he will follow me to the end of the earth. And he has a close friend there in

Kathmandu who knows many people and can help us."

Rachel tells us all these in detail after coming back from dinner. She is excited that Tony is joining us on the trip to Nepal and can't stop talking. She goes on and on, repeating what Tony said several times with joy, telling Jane and me that she is going to Nepal with me, and Tony wants to join us. And he has some friends in Kathmandu who work and volunteer with different organizations and can be of help to us. I have to stop her; otherwise she might go on again.

I say, "It is amazing how everything is falling in place. My angel said, 'Follow your passion, and God will provide all the recourses.'"

With everything Sam told us about his grandfather, I am eager to meet him. I call Sam, asking him to make an appointment with his grandfather. He tells us that in a few days we can go meet him.

After a couple of days, Sam takes Rachel and me to his grandfather's village, which is an easy half-hour drive. He is a tall, charming guy, even at the age of almost ninety years old. He speaks English fluently, since he has studied medicine in London and then has learned the natural healing ways of his ancestors and working with herbs from the elders in his village.

He invites us into his small hut for some herbal tea, saying, "I don't accept many visitors now, but my grandson speaks very highly of you two. He persuaded me to meet with you, and I am also very fond of Jane. Her friends are welcome here."

Then he turns to me, saying, "And I know that you took my advice, so don't be afraid now. Extend your Reach as far as possible. God is with you."

I am dumbstruck, looking at Sam for an explanation of how his grandfather knows about Reach and what advice he is talking about.

Sam says, "I told you he knows everything."

Grandpa continues, "You know my children we are all spirits coming from one source. We are made of energy vibrating with various frequencies. If you have jealousy, hatred, or self-pity in heart, your energy vibration is at its lowest level. But if you feel love and compassion for all beings in heart, your energy vibrates at the highest level and can reach to every corner of the universe. And this doesn't stop just at human level; everything in the world is made of energy, of course, animals and plants but even things that we think are solid and have no life like mountains, rocks, and so on. He takes a deep breath, and pours some-more tea for us, and then continues, this way we can communicate with all things above and below. Just feel the love in your heart; relax, be still, and tap into the energy of the universe. He takes a sip of his tea, looking me in the eye compassionately. I communicate in this way with stars, the moon, and mountains. You already had a glimpse of it, Tara, so don't be frightened. Keep your heart open, keep the ego out of the way, and you will be able to reach the highest corners of all galaxies. In reality the universe is in all of us; there is no distinction. We are one with God and everything."

Again Rachel and I look at Sam, perplexed that he knew about my experience with Mount Kilimanjaro. He continues, "Ego is human's enemy and wants to keep us separate, though we all come to this world as pure spirits. But as we grow and unpleasant things happen, the layers of ego start developing around our true selves in disguise of protection. But when our souls awaken, we become awake to everything we see and hear. So our job is to peel away the layers of ego and self-limitation we impose on ourselves, letting our divine nature shine."

He continues, "I can feel the question of how coming. By meditating and going inside, by praying and giving thanks to God and the universe. And by having compassion for all beings in your heart, also through connecting with others and being of service anywhere you can." And looking at me again, he says, "Follow your heart, my dear; destiny awaits you." And then turning to Rachel, he says, "Your path is of service also but don't lose him—he is your soul mate."

Hugging Rachel and I, he says, "Come for a visit whenever you wish and next time bring Jane too. She is a delightful and loving soul." He kisses Sam on the forehead, saying, "No wonder you are my favorite grandchild. It is because you are wise and have wonderful friends." We leave him with smiles on our faces, and I feel lighter with an unexplainable joy in my heart.

At Jane's place, we invite Sam to have dinner with us. Jane has prepared dinner, and since it is raining, we sit inside around the kitchen table, enjoying the food and wine, telling Jane about the meeting with Sam's grandfather and how loving and wise he is. Rachel is happy, hearing that Tony is her soul mate.

Jane says, "First time visiting Grandpa, I was baffled by how he knew everything and could see deep in my heart. I love that man and don't ever want to lose him."

We discuss the Nepal trip with Sam, explaining the plan to expand our help. Even he is surprised of how his grandfather knew about all that. I say, "Thank your grandpa for us. Maybe we can visit him again after Nepal."

Part 3

NEPAL

The reason why the universe is eternal
is that it does not live for itself, it gives
life to others, as it transforms.

—Lao Tzu

When the Love for Humanity flows, like
a stream in its full strength in our Heart,
no Obstacle can stand on its Way.

In two weeks we are ready for the long journey, not knowing what lies ahead but trusting God and going forward. Jane and Mark take us to the airport, wishing us a safe journey and quick return. Mark has contacted his friend and says he has moved to Patan.

But we have Tony's friend in Kathmandu to connect us with the organization he works for and then can go to Patan.

The flight is long and tiresome, but I have decided to go with the flow and keep an open mind. Rachel is happy, falling sleep on Tony's shoulder. We arrive at Kathmandu's international airport in the evening. Tony's friend Richard is waiting for us after the passport check. Tony makes a quick introduction, saying, "The ladies are tired. Let's go to your home for now. There will be time to get better acquainted later."

Richard has a spacious, clean two-bedroom and two-bathroom apartment with a large living and dining room and kitchen. He invites us to stay at his place as long as we want. He says, "Tony can share my bedroom, and Rachel and you can have the other bedroom."

I say, "Since it is late, we gladly accept the invitation for the night but don't want to impose."

Richard says, "Get some sleep now. We can talk about it tomorrow."

Nepal is landlocked between Tibet from the North and its Eastern, Western, and Southern borders with India. The magnificent Mount Everest, an impressive 29,029 feet above sea level, the tallest mountain on the planet, lies at Nepal's southeast boarder and every year brings hundreds of trekkers to this country. The Nepalese name for Mount Everest is Sagarmatha, which means "Goddess of the Universe." Mount Everest is the highest peak in the Himalayan Mountain range, which spans across the northeastern part of India, passing through the countries of Nepal, Bhutan, China, and some other ones. In addition to the alluring nature, Nepal has many other attractions. There are more than fifty festivals celebrated every year in Nepal, mostly related to the two common religions, Hinduism and Buddhism. These festivals are dedicated to different Hindu and Buddhist gods and goddesses and are celebrated on their special day.

The next morning Rachel and I wake up to the aroma of coffee and a knock at the door; it is Tony. "Hurry up. We are waiting for you to have breakfast." We take quick showers and go to the kitchen.

Tony has prepared a big breakfast, including tomato omelets and toast with butter and jam. He pours coffee for everyone, saying, "Please enjoy, but don't get used to it. From tomorrow I make coffee, but nothing else we have to start our work."

I am hungry since the night before we didn't have dinner, so after thanking Richard and Tony, we sit and enjoy our breakfast with coffee. I think today we have to look for a place to stay during our time in Nepal.

Richard says, "This is my humble abode, as you see. If last night wasn't too uncomfortable, you are welcome to stay. And we can share the expenses of food, water, and whatever else comes up."

We all agree this is the best solution and accept his offer with pleasure. I ask about the women's organization where Richard works to see whether we can help. Richard says he is going to ask his manager, but for the next few days, he suggests that we should take time for some sight-seeing. He says that October and November are the best times to travel to Nepal, and we should take advantage of it before the cold months arrive. He tells us that Kathmandu is a beautiful city and has a lot to offer. He has to go to work; thus, three of us head out to the crowded and noisy streets of Kathmandu.

Nepal has a wet monsoon season and a dry season. The summer (June, July, and August) is hot monsoon season, with rain almost every day and evening thunderstorms. In September, fall, the cooler and dry season starts. October and November are absolutely magnificent with cool, dry weather. And monsoon season just finished, so the flowers are blooming. The countryside is green and lush, and the air is bright and clean.

Kathmandu is the capital and home to Nepal's only international airport. It is a vibrant, crowded city; and like so many capital cities in the developing countries, it has become more congested over the past few years. There is so much history in Kathmandu; you can see modern buildings or Internet cafés developing next to ancient temples. We walk to the old section of town with narrow streets and small shops, where vendors are selling colorful clothing, different knickknacks; and there are spice shops, and their aroma has filled the entire area.

Kathmandu's beautiful Durbar Square is surrounded by historic Buddhist and Hindu temples, but unfortunately many of them are completely destroyed, and some were damaged during the devastating earthquake on April 25,2015. While walking through the streets and squares of Kathmandu, we witness the heartbreaking destruction, but it still has a lot of beautiful and historic sites. We have to dedicate some time to visit all of them. But for now, we are eager to start the work, saying that later there will be time for visiting each of these buildings and temples.

We do some shopping for dinner and go back to the apartment. Tony wants to make dinner to thank Richard for sharing his apartment with us. He makes a delicious meat stew with vegetables. Rachel helps with the salad and sets the table. When Richard comes back, smelling the aroma of the food, he says, "Tony, you are making one of your mom's recipes. I hope it will be as delicious as when she made it." At dinner I ask about the organization where he works and their efforts for helping women.

Richard says, "Lets enjoy our dinner, tony's labor of love that he has worked so hard to prepare. We can talk about the organization and its work over tea, I don't want to make you sad now." The food is delicious, and Rachel and I enjoy listening to Tony and Richard talking about their childhood memories in England.

After dinner Richard makes some tea, and as we sit around the coffee table says, "Women in Nepalese families are treated poorly, particularly in impoverished precincts and villages. They do all the housework, and also have the responsibility of chores outside in the field, carrying heavy loads on their heads. Women usually get less to eat, and if there is any opportunity for education, the boys have priority." He gets up and pours tea for everyone, and continues, "Our director can explain everything better and more clear. She would be happy to see you tomorrow and discus the possibilities for your help."

Richard has been living and working in Kathmandu for the past four years and has traveled to numerous cities and villages all around Nepal. Hence, he has lots of interesting stories to tell, and Rachel and I want to hear it all, but we are tired and sleepy.

Richard says, "In high altitudes you have to get plenty of rest, not exhausting yourself in the first few days but giving your body time to adjust and acclimatize." We say good night and go to our room.

I say, "Sorry, Rachel, that you can't share the room with your green eyes."

"I don't replace my best friend with anyone unless you like to share the room with Richard; he is cute," she answers.

I laugh, saying, "Yes, he is quite handsome, but no thanks. I am happy like this."

The next morning, we wake up to the aroma of coffee and go to the kitchen, more energetic than we were the previous day. Seeing Tony ready to pour the coffee and serve us breakfast, Rachel kisses him over and over, saying, "Is he the best boyfriend or what?"

Richard has already left, but Tony has the address, so after having breakfast, we catch a cab and go to the organization. He drives so fast in the crowded streets that when we arrive, Rachel says her head is spinning. The driving is worse here than in New York.

Richard introduces us to his coworkers and the director of the organization, whose name is Amal. That means "pure and bright" in Nepalese. Amal, who is a kind Nepalese woman in her sixties, welcomes and invites us to her office for tea and pastry.

She tells us that considerable inequality and gender discrimination against women exist in Nepal, though the government and women's right groups are trying to change that, "Women are subordinate to men since the society is mostly patriarchal in Nepal. They work harder and longer hours than men but get less to eat. So malnutrition and poverty hit women much more. In low-income families and villages, girls have limited or no access to education and health care. Girls as young as seven years old are forced to marry or sold to men much older. There are a high number of child abuse and rape victims. As you see, the need for help is vast and urgent." Amal gets up and pours some tea and serves us some pastry, and says, "Our organization works in different facets. We provide education for girls and also married women of every age so they can get better jobs. In our education centers, we also teach them working skills like sewing, tailoring, handloom weaving, and some business aspects of handling money. Cases of domestic violence are frequently reported to us by neighbors or other family members. The husbands beat their wives and children, injuring them without feeling any remorse. We visit the family and try to help by providing psychological consultation to both husband and wife. And if that doesn't work and the husband continues the violent behavior, we give legal assistance to women for their rights." Amal asks about our interests, and what brought us to Nepal.

Rachel and I talk about our charity Reach and the work we are doing in Tanzania. I tell Amal the reason for our tip to Nepal and our desire to expand the aid to several countries. We discuss the ways Reach can help. Amal tells us we can go to the center anytime we wish, helping with legal cases. She says we should also have fun while in Nepal and take time to do some sight-seeing in Kathmandu.

Richard decides to join for lunch and then shows us around. Kathmandu, a multiethnic, crowded, and noisy city, is the capital of Nepal with many points of attraction. Richard takes us to a traditional Nepalese restaurant. Nepalese cuisine varies with the region, and some meals are similar to Indian foods but healthier with less fat, leaner meat, and big chunks of fresh vegetables. He orders a few different dishes, such as dal, which is yellow, or red lentil soup with spices served over rice; there are also meat kebabs and spicy potato-and-pea salad for us to try.

We enjoy the food and then walk toward the Durbar Square with its temples and palaces. It was also famously called Basantapur or Hanuman Durbar Square and is a UNESCO World Heritage Site. Located in front of Kathmandu's royal palace, this spectacular Durbar Square demonstrates the impressive artistry that existed in the past. Sadly, some of the temples and historic buildings have been destroyed in the devastating earthquake. But there are still enough left that one can admire and enjoy the craftsmanship and details used in the architecture. Richard tells us Durbar Square was surrounded by spectacular buildings, which vividly showcased the skill of artisans over many centuries, and it is extremely sad to see some of these sites demolished. There are Buddhist and Hindu temples we want to visit, but we decide to leave them for another day and walk to Richard's apartment.

Tony says he is going to make dinner for us again. Rachel is surprised. "Since when did you become such a chef?"

"My parents own a few restaurants in Liverpool, and during my college years, I sometimes worked there. They wanted me to take over the business, but I had other passions." Richard says that during his college years, he would go to their restaurant frequently for a free meal.

Richard opens a bottle of red wine, and while Tony is preparing the food, we sit around the kitchen table, enjoying the wine and planning for the rest of our time in Nepal. I ask Richard whether he knows Mark's friend Jack. He says, "Yes, I know him, and we often got together when he lived in Kathmandu, but now Jack lives in Patan."

"We have to manage our time carefully," I say, "since there is a lot to do before leaving Nepal. We want to visit some villages and also go to Patan to visit Jack, who volunteers for another women's organization that works against human trafficking."

The next morning, we go to Richard's work, discussing with Amal the ways we can help in Nepal. Amal suggests that we provide funds for a new educational center for married women and young girls, and a day care in case any of them have children. The center will be under Reach charity, but since we don't live in Nepal, she can manage the work. Rachel and I say we have to talk it over with the other board members, but surely it would be possible.

Amal knows the organization in Patan where Jack works. She says, "They are a group of brave women and men trying to stop human trafficking and help the rescued victims. I am certain they will appreciate any help that you can provide."

In few days, we are ready to go to Patan. Richard offers to drive us there, saying he hasn't seen Jack for a while and would like to pay him a visit. Early morning, after getting our coffee, we are in the car, ready. The scenery on the way is beautiful, and the short drive goes smoothly.

Patan City, also known as Lalitpur, is situated on the southern bank of the holy Bagmati River, about five kilometers southeast of Kathmandu. It has now become practically part of sub-metropolitan Kathmandu. The city is famous for its wealth of Buddhist and Hindu temples. With an abundance of fine bronze gateways and wonderful carvings, it is a cultural heritage. Patan is known for its expert artists and metal workers, and is enclosed within four stupas, which are said to have been built in the third century AD by Emperor Ashoka. A stupa is a hemispherical structure containing relics from Buddhist monks and nuns. It is the oldest Buddhist monument used as a shrine to dead, and now has evolved into a place for honoring the living and for practicing meditation.

When we arrive at Jack's apartment, he and Richard exchange a friendly hug and some British jokes only they understand and laugh at. Jack greets us warmly, inviting everyone in for tea and rice cookies, saying he was expecting us sooner since Mark had informed him of our visit. He serves tea and cookie, and Rachel and I tell him a little about ourselves and the Reach organization. Then I ask him about the group he works with and their projects.

Jack says, "We have a lot to discuss, and it can't be done in a few hours. If you stay for a few days, we will have time to talk about the situation of women and girls and our efforts to help them. You are welcome to stay at my place. I have a guest room."

Richard says he has to go back but will return whenever we want. Tony kisses Rachel, saying he is going with Richard so old friends can spend a few days together without girls. Rachel says, "Be careful what you wish for, Tony. I might let you be without me forever."

Tony kisses her and says, "I will never, ever want to be without you, but there will be just a few days to be with my old body, talking about our childhood memories and our school years."

Rachel laughs and says, "Go now. We have work to do. I forgive you."

After Richard and Tony leave, Jack takes us for a walk around Patan, saying we can talk about work at night over dinner. We enjoy the walk, admiring the impressive allure of the different temples, though many of them were demolished during the earthquake of April 2015. I say, "If we have time, it would be great to visit some of these temples."

At Jack's place, we help prepare some salad and simple food with whatever ingredient he has, then sit around the kitchen table, enjoying the meal and our new friendship.

Jack says, "I should have made a better, more complete, meal for your first night in my place, especially since Mark has asked me to take good care of you."

Rachel and I thank him for his hospitality and kindness in inviting us to stay and saying we like simple food. After dinner Jack puts on some tea and starts telling us about the work he and his coworkers do.

He says, "Human trafficking is a big problem in Nepal, every year about five to ten thousand women and young girls between the ages of seven and twenty-four are trafficked from Nepal to India for forced labor or sex slavery in brothel houses, and the number is alarmingly increasing. Domestic violence, poverty, rape, illiteracy, and lack of education are the factors contributing to this increase. Human traffickers are like predators, going to different villages and looking for opportunities to influence and lure innocent, vulnerable girls. They abduct the girls by force and then drug them or by promise of a well-paying job and the potential of marring a wealthy businessman so they can support their entire family."

"The most in danger and easily controlled are the ones with abusive fathers or brothers and the girls who were raped and are ashamed to come forward. Sometimes even due to extreme poverty, the fathers sell their daughters for a little money."

Taking a sip of his tea, Jack continues, "In our organization we take action against this problem from several angles, the most crucial being raising awareness about this colossal issue facing humanity. We identify the villages that are more susceptible to trafficking. Our group travels to these areas, informing the parents and girls about these criminals and the ways they work. We ask them to be aware of the strangers coming to their villages, attempting to seduce the girls. And we encourage them to immediately alert the authorities about these suspicious people."

"We provide education, teaching them reading and writing while trying to reduce the rate of illiteracy in small cities and villages. In our education centers, women and girls can also learn practical skills like tailoring, candle making, child care, and other expertise to get better jobs and become independent. The organization has few safe houses in villages where the rescued victims of trafficking can stay for a few months to a year. In these centers, we provide psychological and legal assistance to these women and girls while teaching them various income-generating skills, building their confidence and self-esteem."

Rachel and I listen attentively and think of the ways we can help. It is late, so Jack shows us the guest room, saying that the next day we can go to the organization together.

The next morning, we wake up very early, and after the meditation—to my joyous surprise, Rachel has been faithfully participating—we go to the kitchen and sit with Jack for breakfast and coffee. I ask about his friendship with Mark. Jack tells us he and Mark are childhood friends and went to school and college together. After obtaining their degree in psychology, Mark wanted to summit Mount Kilimanjaro, but Jack had the desire to come to Nepal and study meditation in one of the monasteries here.

He says, "You know the rest of the story about Mark, and as for me, during that time, I became friends with a group of doctors who travel to Nepal every year, treating patients in villages. I sensed this calling that I should stay here and help. Seeing the condition of women and girls, and also hearing about trafficking broke my heart, and I felt this is what I want to help with. I talked to the director of the organization; she accepted me gladly. I give psychological assistance in several centers and once a year travel to England for doing some fund-raising. You will meet our director today; she is a kind and humble but amazingly powerful woman."

"It is still early, so let's go out for a morning walk, enjoying this cool, fresh, and crisp air."

We ask Jack if it is possible to visit a Buddhist temple and a Hindu temple.

"We can go to Durbar Square this afternoon or tomorrow morning; there are many historic monuments and temples we can enjoy visiting," he says. "You know Patan was always known for its fine arts and crafts, the wood and stone carvings, metal statues, elaborate architecture, including more than a dozen Hindu and Buddhist temples. So there is a lot to see; if you stay for few more days, we will have time. Let's go to the women's organization, and depending on how our meeting with the manager goes, we will decide. Patan is a small town and easy to walk everywhere."

The work day has already started at the center when we get there. Jack introduces Rachel and me, asking one of his coworkers to take us to the director's office, since he is late for one of the abused girl's therapy sessions. I expected the director to be a Nepalese lady, but to our surprise, when she opens the door, we see this attractive woman in her fifties welcoming us with a heavy French accent.

Bernadette is from Grenoble, France, and is one the founders, and director of this women's organization. She explains their mission and approach to solving the problem of human trafficking. She tells us there are posts along the border of India, and sometimes the traffickers get caught, and the women and girls are rescued, but it is a long border with little control.

"After the earthquake, the issue regarding human trafficking got worse, and the number increased since many children lost both or one of their parents and became more vulnerable. In rare occasions, the girls run away and come back to Nepal; they are the physically and mentally strong ones. But escaping from that situation, they are traumatized and need plenty of physical and psychological help." She continues after a brief pause, "We provide safe houses, giving them education and skills to work and become autonomous—also health care, psychological therapy, and legal assistant if needed."

I ask what brought Bernadette to Nepal, living in Patan. She pours some tea and serves cookies; she starts her story.

"When I was five years old, my parents died in a car accident, which left me alone and devastated, not understanding the severity of the situation. I was at my grandparents' when the accident occurred, so I kept asking my grandmother why my parents had left me and when they would come back. She had just lost her daughter and was sorrowful beyond measure but was trying to console me. Though my grandparents were kind and loving, I cried all night, asking when my parents would be back. I felt abandoned and lost, thinking they left because they didn't love me. My grandfather was telling me that was not true, and they loved me very much and would always be with me in my heart. He would explain to me that my parents were in heaven and would watch over me. But I didn't want to accept that and was waiting every day and night for them to come take me home. The weeping and begging my parents to come back went on for about six months."

"One night I saw a beautiful angel in a dream, holding me and saying that my parents were with God but love me and watch over me all the time. Immediately a warm and comfortable feeling went through my entire body, enveloping me with love. And putting my head on the angel's shoulder as she was holding me, I sobbed for a long time. Then she kissed me, saying that I will do great things in the world, and can call her whenever I need guidance. From that night on, I didn't cry anymore and realized my parents would never come back but were watching me from heaven. I grew up at my grandparents' place and went to school. I loved traveling and exploring, so I studied archaeology and got my master's degree. I had forgotten about my angel encounter till years later; it was during a devastating divorce that she appeared in my dream again, consoling me. I worked with a group traveling to different countries for expeditions." She stops for few seconds and then says, "Seven years ago, we took an expedition trip to Nepal, going to different archaeological sites. I met a lady name Amal, who is the director of a woman's charity in Kathmandu. She talked about the condition of women and girls in Nepal."

I interrupt her, saying, "We have been to that women's charity and are going to work with them."

Bernadette continues, "And visiting different villages, I heard horrible tales of young women and girls being trafficked, which saddened me deeply. I wanted to do something for them. Back in France, I kept thinking about the women and girls stolen or lured into trafficking and wanted to help them. I could feel their loneliness and fear in my heart, so I prayed, asking the angel for guidance, and she responded. 'You are on the right path. Go to Nepal and help those innocent girls. God is with you.' I talked to my friends and started this organization. I traveled between France and Nepal for more than a year, but we needed a director to live here mostly. I am divorced and have no children, and my grandparents passed away many years ago. I have no close family in France. My friends and board members asked me, and I accepted the call to move to Patan and love it here."

"I think Jack has told you about the diversity of the work our organization does to help the women, trying to eradicate, or at least decrease, the amount of trafficking. If you like, we can visit one of our safe houses where we have a few girls who have escaped recently. You can talk to one of them, and I will translate. I have learned the Nepalese language, but we also have a translator."

We appreciate the opportunity to talk to one of the girls, so we will go for a visit tomorrow morning. Bernadette says, "Now you tell me. What has brought you to Nepal?"

Rachel and I tell her about Reach charity and the desire to collaborate with them. Bernadette says, "Since you aren't going to stay here, take one of the projects and provide the funds for it. This way you can come for a visit whenever possible." I think it's a great idea, and, consulting with Rachel, we agree on building another safe house if Bernadette and her coworkers can bring the staff.

We hear a knock at the door; it is Jack, saying, "Aren't you ladies hungry? It is three in the afternoon."

We ask Bernadette to join us for lunch, but she has work to do and apologizes for talking so long. She invites us to dinner the next evening at her apartment, saying we have a lot more to talk about.

We go for a walk and enjoy early dinner at a restaurant Jack knows. The owner, Ram, a friend of Jack's from Patan, greets us, asking whether he can order some specialty food for us. He sits with us, talking about Patan and saying that the real name is Lalitpur, meaning "city of beauty." And with its elaborate artwork and details used in the temples, it really is a beautiful city.

"There are more than fifty festivals celebrated every year in Patan," Ram says. "For your next trip, try to be here in September and October; those are the times for most of the Buddhist and Hindu festivals. Though your time is limited, try to visit the Buddhist Golden Temple."

The next day after breakfast, we go to the center with Jack. Bernadette and another lady, the translator, are waiting to take us to one of their safe houses. It is a short walk, and when we get there, girls are all in different classes. Some are studying reading, writing, and math; and the others are learning arts and various crafts.

We talk to the manager of this safe house, and she tells us the girls are happy and comfortable in the house. But most of them have some kind of psychological problem, because of the horrors they have been through. They are physically and psychologically traumatized. They wake up in the middle of the night, screaming, due to having horrible nightmares and are afraid to fall back sleep.

I ask if we can talk to the girls who recently escaped from a brothel in India. She says there are four of them who came here a few months ago; three of them are timid and afraid of strangers. But there is one girl who has an amazingly strong spirit, and that is how she could save herself and three other girls. We go to one of the rooms and wait; after five minutes the manager comes back with a petite girl, saying, "This is Atal. That means 'unshakable,' and she truly is that."

She says hi and hugs us without any hesitation or shyness. Bernadette kisses her and asks some questions we don't understand. I want to know her story from the beginning, so our translator asks her, and this is what she says.

"I lived in a small village on the border of India with my parents and two brothers. My father was a serious and difficult man, but I had a kind, caring, and hardworking mother. I loved to go to school and learn everything, and though at first my father was against it, finally with my mother's effort, he agreed. When I was twelve, one day while walking to our little school, I saw two men following me. I started running, but they grabbed me, and while one of them was holding me down, the other one put a shawl on my face, and everything went black."

"I woke up with a headache in the back of a truck, not knowing what had happened. The air was heavy and I could feel others press against my body from both side. Looking around after that, my eyes got used to the darkness. I saw about twenty girls between the age of seven and eighteen and ten boys around the same ages. We were cramped together with little air to breathe. Some were crying, and others looked completely terrified and in shock."

"I tried to be calm and assess the situation. Our teacher had told us about people who kidnap and sell you, so I thought this must be it, not realizing what was awaiting ahead. Right then and there, I made two promises to God and myself. The first one was that no matter what happens, I will not lose my faith in God and will not let them break my spirit or bring me down. The second was that I will escape and come back home in spite of how hard or how far it may be. Making that decision, I felt a spark of light in my heart and started to console the younger kids who were horrified, calling their mothers and crying."

"In some parts the road was bumpy throwing us around on top of each-other. I don't know for how long we were in that dark and tight space till the truck stopped; a man opened the back door and motioned us to get out. I rubbed my eyes to be able to see after being in the darkness, and jumped down. They put us in a row, and another man came out of the building and, looking at us carefully, pointed at some of us. He picked all the younger girls and a few boys, and the rest of the boys, with a few girls who were about eighteen, were pushed back in the truck. Then he drove away. Can you imagine how it felt, not knowing where that was and why we were taken? The little girls started sobbing loud again." Atal wipes the tears from the corners of her eyes and holds Bernadette's hand, like she is looking for support.

Then taking a deep breath she goes on, "They took us inside. As we were passing a long hallway, we saw other young girls staring at us with emotionless eyes. And when one of them started talking, the man who was moving behind, pushing us like a herd of sheep, slapped her on the face, saying, 'No talking.' Words cannot describe my emotions. I was angry, sad, frustrated, and scared but didn't want them to see any fear on my face, since that is how they control the girls: by terrorizing them."

"I tell you, it is the worst feeling in the world when your most essential human right, which is freedom, is taken away without any reason or justification. You feel violated, helpless, and disrespected in your body and soul. But this was nothing compared to what was awaiting us ahead. We were led to a room, and then an older woman came and explained our duty, which was obeying everything she said if we wanted to stay alive and get any food."

"We were obligated to sleep with as many men as they asked us to, and to let them do whatever they wanted to do with us. That night I cried till morning, and praying, I reinforced my promises. Our work started on the next day. I was a virgin and frightened, but I made a choice to act wisely and plan for an escape."

"At night, the little girls were sobbing and wanting to go home. I would hold them in my arms, telling stories and asking them to be patient. I became friends with the head woman and got some little privileges for us. I asked for some books and permission to teach reading and writing to the girls after our work. We were watched closely, and after one year, I hadn't yet found the way to get out of there. I had seen the girls who disobeyed the boss being beaten to death. I had cautiously talked to a few girls about planning our escape, and every night I would pray to God to show me the way, trying to keep my spirit up. Almost two years passed, much longer than I wanted to stay. But any plans I made they would find out, and we would get beaten hard."

"Every few months some new girls were brought the same way as us. A truck would stop, leave the devastated and shocked girls, and then drive away with the rest. I had a friendly relation with all the girls, the workers, and the boss lady. The girls looked up to me and would listen to my advice." Atal stops again, remembering those horrible memories must be extremely difficult for her. Feeling her agony saddens me, so I ask if she is tired and wants to tell us the rest of the events another day.

But she likes to continue, "One day a man came and asked for me, but when we were in the room, he didn't want to have sex and just wanted to talk. He said he could help and get me out of that horrible house, but I didn't want to leave without the four other girls who were part of the escape plan. First, he hesitated, saying, 'There is no room in my car,' but finally I convinced him. He said to be ready that very night and to get out at midnight when everybody was asleep and walk to the end of the alley, where he would be waiting for us. Then he paid for the fee and left."

"I wasn't sure if he could be trusted, but it was our only chance to get out of there. I rushed and found the other girls, telling them what the guy had said. We were five girls who had planned to escape; we were all around the same age except one who was eighteen. After our last client and dinner, I saw the doorkeeper locking the door and hanging the key. They were all sleeping, but the five of us were just pretending to be sleep."

"At midnight I quietly sneaked in the door man's room and took the key. My heart was beating so fast, almost jumping out of my chest. The girls were ready, waiting at the door, but the eighteen-year-old at the last moment had changed her mind. I talked to her, asking the reason for not wanting to leave. She said, 'I was stolen and brought here at the age of eight and now at eighteen have nowhere to go, and no one would want me. I don't have any news from my parents and don't even know if they are alive. I know nothing from the outside world and am scared to go out.' Then she hugged me, wishing us good luck, and went back to bed. And this is the saddest thing that happens in these houses. After some time, the girls completely lose their hope and true identity. And that degrading humiliation becomes their reality, thinking this is who they really are. And that was the worst fact that troubled me, and I didn't want it to happen. So I had to free myself and as many girls as possible, no matter what would happen."

"We didn't have much time, so we opened the door quietly and stepped out. I took a deep breath and started running with the three other girls. We ran as fast as we could, not looking back or catching our breath till I saw the car at the end of the alley. The guy who I believe was an angel sent by God to save us got out of the car, opened the door, and motioned us to hurry. We got in the car, and he pressed the gas pedal so hard that the car jumped and flew away. With every meter of distance between us and that horrible place, I could breathe easier. The three other runaways were shaking and holding on to me."

"I couldn't tell how many hours he was driving quietly without any word or explanation for taking such a dangerous risk. If the men running the house caught him or any of us, they would have killed us without hesitation. The other girls fell asleep, but I was watching our savior, wondering who that was. Then he said, 'I will drive to Nepal and near your village, but from there you have to walk home and never look back or ask about me.' I thanked him and asked his name, but he didn't answer. After some more driving, it was almost dawn when he stopped, saying, 'This is where we separate, but I will watch to make sure you are safely home.' We got out and started walking fast, looking around to see if someone was following us."

Atal pauses again looking at each-one of us with teary eyes, and holding on tighter to Bernadette, starts with a sigh, "We didn't thank him properly, and I don't even know his name. Almost three years had passed, and we didn't know how our parents would react to seeing us. All the other girls were afraid of their father and didn't want to go home. We walked to my parents' house and waited in a corner until my father and brothers left for work. I walked to the door slowly; my legs were shaking, and my heart was beating fast. I was excited to see my mother but didn't know how she would receive me. She opened the door, and, seeing me, she almost passed out but kept herself up and just stared at my face for few moments, like she wanted to make sure it was in fact I who was standing in front of her. Then she grabbed me, holding tight, and let her tears roll down her face. I called the other girls, and we went inside. In three years, she had aged more than twenty years. She didn't ask any questions and wouldn't want to know anything about the past three years."

"We were hungry and exhausted. My mother prepared some food for us and, while we were eating, said, 'You can't stay here. Your father and brothers said that our family was dishonored when you were taken. They invented a story that you were killed in an accident. Now if they see you back, your father will kill you to save the family honor. When you and the other girls were taken, the entire village was in despair and sorrow. The men searched for weeks, but at the end the families had to accept that their girls were gone. The thought of you being in those places was unbearable for your father; thus, he created the story of you being killed. He believed that and didn't want to hear otherwise.' Then she continues, saying, 'I have heard about an organization in Patan that helps girls like you. Finish your food, get some rest, and I will take you there before your father and brothers come back.'"

"I had missed my family and wanted to see them but knew that there was no other way. That day my mother brought us here and before leaving hugged me and, kissing my face over and over, said, 'You are my only daughter, and I want you to live free and have a wonderful life. You are strong and can do whatever you want, so put everything that has happened in the past three years behind you and never look back or think about it. Go to school and make a better life for yourself. Don't let the past three years hold you back in life. They have no power over you. Just go forward with faith and courage. My love and prayers are always with you but don't come back home or to our village again.' And with that she walked away, wiping her tears."

"That was the last time I saw my mother. You see, when these criminals take the girls, they don't just destroy our lives but our families as well. We were four girls stolen from the same village, and as my mother told us, our whole community was devastated and destroyed by this tragedy. I can never see my father and brothers again."

"Now I am determined to study and become a lawyer to help the other girls and boys who are taken from their homes. Madam Bernadette has promised me to help the other girls that were in the house, trying to free them. And she has promised to send me to other schools to become a lawyer." She pauses and then says, "Would you help those girls, too, please?"

I look at her with awe, wiping my tears, and, looking at Rachel, notice that she is crying also. Bernadette says they are trying to tackle this issue, but the problem is huge and needs collaboration of all the countries involved and a big fund. I hug and kiss Atal, saying, "We will do every effort possible to assist you and other girls."

She says, "You are my friend. Now please come back for another visit."

She is so innocent but has an incredibly high spirit. We promise to come back and see her on our next trip to Nepal and leave. Hearing her story makes my heart and soul ache. I had heard sad stories about human trafficking but never firsthand like this from someone who has lived it, and has escaped.

"And you haven't heard nothing yet. There are much worse stories that we hear and see," says Bernadette. "And she didn't want to go through a lot of awful details that she had told us before."

We meet Jack and go back to his apartment, but I can't stop thinking about Atal and all the other girls and boys, the victims of human trafficking, wanting to help them.

The next day we get our coffee early and head out to Durbar Square for visiting the Golden Temple. This unique Buddhist monastery, amazingly untouched by the earthquake, is a UNESCO World Heritage Site and gets its name from the gilded facade and golden statues around it. It was founded in the twelfth century, and it has existed in its current form since 1409. Two large elephant statues guard the temple's doorway.

Jack tell us we have to walk clockwise around the temple, so that is what we do.

We admire the grace and the skill used in every detail. Then we go in for prayer and meditation. We sit for a long meditation, enjoying the serenity of the silence. I have an amazing experience going deep and feel myself floating over the clouds and eventually coming back, hearing Jack and Rachel talking.

In the evening, we walk with Jack to Bernadette's home for dinner. She opens the door, inviting us into her meticulously decorated apartment, which instantly lifts the spirit. One can feel a high vibration of joy and peace everywhere. Bernadette, noticing our amazement, says, "I love art and beauty, so I surround myself with my souvenirs from traveling around the world. The monetary value of objects isn't important to me but the history and feelings put into it. Some of the artifacts from my trips were broken during the earthquake, and the building was damaged, but thankfully we didn't lose anyone."

She gives us a tour of her three-bedroom apartment, saying, "Being tidy and clean saves us time and is good for the soul. Our vibration and energy affect our environment, including everyone and everything in it. This way we can raise or bring down other people's energy. We go back to the family room, and Bernadette pours the red wine she has opened to breathe, offering us some appetizers. We sit on the sofa, sip the wine, and talk about our lives like we have been close friends for years."

I'd like to talk about Atal and what we can do for her, but Bernadette says, "No sad stories tonight. We shouldn't let these horrible stories of cruelty that exist in the world, bring us down. In the contrary they make us stronger and more determined to reach out, and help others with total commitment."

After a few glasses of wine, we are tipsy, laughing silly. Bernadette says, "I should serve dinner before being totally drunk." She prepared a green salad and sautéed chicken with lemon and garlic. We sit around the kitchen table, enjoying the delicious food and the second bottle of wine till past midnight.

Bernadette says, "Next time you should spend more time in Patan and stay in my place, and I have a small villa in Grenoble that we can go to sometimes for vacation." Then, laughing, she says, "Sorry, Jack. You can join us, too."

We hug and thank her for the incredible hospitality and wonderful night. Outside, the cold midnight breeze of November gets rid of any remaining tipsiness. The next morning we wake up around eight o'clock in the morning.

We take cold showers to clear our heads, and, sitting at the kitchen table, we enjoy the extra-strong coffee Jack has made. We walk to the women's center with Jack.

Rachel and I go to Bernadette's office to discuss the plan for building another safe house for rescued or escapee women and girls. Bernadette says she is going to find a suitable building or land so they can build a house, which would be a better solution. We agree, asking her to estimate the cost and send us a proposal for showing to the other board members.

Tony and Richard are coming to take us to Kathmandu in the afternoon, so we kiss Bernadette and her coworkers, saying we will be in touch. Bernadette says, "I will miss you, so come again soon and also reserve a date for the trip to France."

We walk back with Jack to his apartment. Tony and Richard have arrived and are sitting in the car, waiting for us. Tony jumps out, hugging and kissing Rachel ten times or maybe more. We thank Jack, hoping to see him soon. He promises to take a trip to Kathmandu to see us before we leave Nepal. Tony and Richard want to know everything about our stay in Patan. We tell them about Bernadette and the organization's work against girl trafficking.

Rachel says, "How was your guy time alone? Did you miss us?"

Tony and Richard look at each other and laugh, but before Rachel can open her mouth to object, Tony says, "Of course I missed you every second."

At Richard's apartment, Tony volunteers to make dinner for us. And of course that is because the three of us have been lazy, taking advantage of his willingness to do the cooking. And when he asks for help, Rachel tells him, "But my love, you are so good and fast that we wouldn't want to mess with your process."

The next morning, we go to Richard's work with him, eager to see Amal and tell her all about our stay in Patan. She welcomes us back, and we go to her office for tea and some pastry, which is always part of the meetings. We discuss our meeting with Bernadette and our collaboration. I say that our departure from Nepal is coming up, and we have to make sure everything is in order before leaving. Amal says, "I want you to meet a dear friend of mine who lives in a small village not very far from Kathmandu. He is a wonderful, attractive Italian man I have known for a very long time."

Rachel says, "In that case we absolutely want to meet him."

In the evening before going home, Amal asks whether we are ready to go the next morning to visit Piero. She can come with a driver to Richard's place to pick us up early in the morning.

We drink the strong coffee Tony has made with some toast and get ready, waiting for Amal. Richard has some appointment at work and can't join us. So Tony, Rachel, and I get in the car with Amal and the driver, who is a polite young boy from Kathmandu. He drives us through a narrow dirt road for almost an hour and then stops, opening the car door.

Rachel says, "Oh good, we arrived at the village."

Amal says, "No, we did not, but there is no more road, so from here we have to go by mule or walk."

Rachel and I look at each other and say, "We walk." But Tony wants to go by mule.

Rachel says, "Tony, you are too heavy for this poor mule."

We have to walk or hike up a steep road for more than an hour. The altitude is higher, and the thinner air makes breathing hard.

Finally, we arrive at a small village. We see women carrying huge loads on their heads with their kids on their backs, walking fast. Some kids are playing in the road.

Amal stops in front of a tiny house and knocks. An old man opens the door and, hugging Amal, invites us in with a big, almost toothless smile. His wrinkled face radiates love, and his eyes shine with joy. He introduces himself, and Amal tells him about Rachel, Tony, and me.

Piero pours tea for us and serves some cake, saying that he made it himself. He sits next to me and asks the purpose of our trip to Nepal. Is it vacation, work, or something else? I tell him about Reach organization and our work in Tanzania and the desire to expand it to Nepal. Rachel talks a little about our plans here, and the work we are going to do with Amal and Bernadette.

"As the great Indian sage Patanjali says, 'When you are inspired by some great purpose and some extraordinary project, all your thoughts break their bonds. Your mind transcends limitations, your consciousness expands in every direction, and you find yourself in a new, great, and wonderful world. Dormant forces, faculties, and talents become alive, and you discover yourself to be a greater person by far than you ever dreamed yourself to be,'" Piero says.

"Therefore, if you have aspired to help and serve, follow your heart, and you will be amazed by your strength and capabilities, achieving goals that you never thought possible before." He continues, saying, "As long as people like you exist, there is hope for humanity."

Tony asks about his life and what brought him to this small village on top of a steep hill. Piero says he is originally from Florence, Italy; and after obtaining his master's degree in marketing, he started his own import/export company in Rome and made a big fortune at very young age. When he was thirty years old, he got married to a beautiful girl from a wealthy family, who were friends of his parents. He says they were living in a large villa in the suburbs of Rome and had three children: two boys and one girl.

He continues his story, "We were happy with no worries in the world till some years later our daughter started losing weight. She was always tired and couldn't play with other kids. Finally, at the age of thirteen, she was diagnosed with leukemia, and that shattered our lives into a million pieces."

"We took her to the best specialists and clinics all around the world, giving her all the possible care. One of my sons was a match for bone marrow, so the doctors did the operation. My daughter got better and could continue her school, and we were happy again. But the disease came back, and after five years of battling and suffering, she passed away. She had just turned eighteen and was getting ready for college. All those years she was the one with high spirit, giving us hope and courage. She never complained and was always smiling with a joyful attitude like she knew something we didn't."

"After her passing, my wife fell into a deep depression and started taking strong medication. I did everything in my power to help her, but nothing worked. Our sons were both in college and needed my attention. They were devastated from losing their sister and seeing their mother like that. So I had to be strong for them, taking care of my wife and attending to every aspect of our lives. With the suggestion of a dear friend, I enrolled in a meditation and yoga class; in seeing the benefits, I made it a daily practice. I tried to take my wife to the course, but she didn't want to even hear about it. I had to focus on our sons so they could have a healthy and happy life. Now they are both doctors. My older boy is a cardiologist, and the younger is a psychiatrist. They are happily married, and each has two kids."

I ask about his wife. Piero wipes the tear from his wrinkled face, takes a deep sigh, and says she committed suicide. "One day, coming back from work, I found her in a bathtub full of blood. She had cut her wrist."

The room becomes completely quiet, as if we weren't even breathing. After a few minutes, Piero says he couldn't continue his life and work like before anymore. He sold the huge house and put money aside for his sons' education and invested some for their future. He says, "I don't want to tire you with my life story."

But we all say, "No, please continue."

So, after catching his breath, he says, "I was sad beyond measure and kept thinking about the meaning of this life and couldn't understand why those things had happened to my family. So I closed my office and started on a journey, wanting to find some meaning and purpose in life. I went to Tibet and lived in a monastery for five years, studying Buddhism and meditating for hours every day."

"One day deep in my meditation, I felt my entire body was lifted with a surge of high energy, and my heart emanated a bright light. I saw the face of Divine in my heart and felt an amazing love going through my veins and every cell. Following that my heart started softening. I didn't constantly think of my sadness and misery. But on the contrary, I felt an inexplicable joy in my heart and saw beauty in everything. I wanted to help and serve others in need."

"See, my children, compassion causes the heart to expand and become universal. Thus, never let your heart become cold. It limits your true potential. I heard my calling to serve and left the monastery and went on a walking journey through India. Passing from village to village, seeing the hungry and ill-looking kids, I felt my heart melting with love and empathy. It seemed like I was connected to them, feeling their pain and hunger. I felt connected with everyone and everything in the world. I could feel and talk to animals, plants, stars, moon, and ultimately God and angels."

"In one of the villages along my way, I saw kids in the worst condition and wanted to do something to help. I found an organization that was already helping there and provided the funds for building two safe houses for homeless kids: one for girls and one for boys. I continued my journey to Nepal, stayed in Kathmandu for some time, and met this wonderful lady, Amal. We became friends sharing the same passion for helping others."

"One day we walked to this village, and it immediately felt like home. I bought a small land and built this house, and I have been living here for almost twenty years now. Children are curious and want to learn, but there was no school here, and in brutal winter weather, they had to sit outside during class hours. I built a school here and then a few more in other villages that had the same condition."

"When we get out of our ego self and little me, opening and expanding our hearts, raising our vibrational energy with love and joy, the universe opens up to us, and we become one with all. To change our lives and contribute to others, first, we have to change our thoughts and the way of looking at events and occurrences. As Lao Tzu has said, 'If you correct your mind, the rest of your life will fall into place.'"

He continues, "We have to find the positive in every situation. You see, my children, happiness is a choice and should not depend on external circumstances. Feel life as the ultimate gift that is and see the miracles and joy in everything. Observe the miracle in the smile of a little kid, in sunshine, in colorful clouds, in a sunset, or in sharing a cup of tea and conversation with friends. Nature can be an amazing teacher to us if we pay attention and tune in to its energy. Every little particle in nature vibrates with energy. If we look inside a flower or rock, we would see a bright light spinning like a shining sun. So take a walk in nature; connect with it by raising your vibrational energy to the level of love and light. This way you can communicate with anything in the world, even other galaxies and dimensions. Ask any questions and receive the answer. So choose the energy of love, open your heart with compassion, and be joyful now, showing gratitude for all the blessings in life."

He continues, "I still walk and hike for hours every day, visiting villages and connecting with people to find out how I can help and be of service to them."

He asks if we would like to go visit the school, so we walk with him to the small building with few classrooms. The minute he enters a class, all kids gather around, hugging him with big smiles. He hugs and kisses each one of them, asking some questions about their studies.

Walking out, he says, "These are all my children, and I love them deeply."

He asks us to visit him again if our time permits. We thank him and leave with a sense of admiration for his inexhaustible energy. Rachel says he is a thoroughly commendable man, but I wouldn't put him in the attractive category.

Laughing, Amal replies, "I didn't mean his appearance, though when younger, he was quite a catch. But you should have met him in spirit, Rachel, to see how beautiful he really is."

I understand what Amal means and feel we did connect in our hearts and souls. We walk down the hill, where the driver is waiting in the car to take us back to the center. We talk to Richard and the ladies there about our amazing and inspiring experience with Piero.

In the evening, Tony says he is tired of cooking and that we should go out for dinner. We walk to a restaurant Richard suggests, saying the food is fresh and healthy. Then we walk to a cozy café for espresso and dessert. It is a small space packed with people of all ages and nationalities: tourists, hikers, and also locals. We sit at a table in the corner and order coffee and some pastries.

A group of American hikers, as they introduce themselves, approach our table and start talking to us. They ask about the purpose of our trip and whether we are also in Nepal for hiking. Tony, trying to get rid of them, just says we aren't hikers. But one of the guys, who ironically is called John, insists on talking to me alone.

"I don't want to be rude, but as you see, we are having a private conversation," Tony says. But the guy doesn't give up, saying that maybe the next day we could go out for coffee or a drink. As I refuse, Rachel kicks me so hard under the table that she makes me jump with pain. But, keeping my composure, I say we are leaving Nepal in a few days and that there is no time.

Then Richard, holding my arm, says, "Let's leave before that john comes back." Outside he grasps my arm tightly while Tony and Rachel hold hands, walking ahead of us.

In our room, as we are getting ready for bed, Rachel wants to know what my conversation with Richard was and what he told me. I explain that we are just friends and were talking about work and nothing more.

She says, "Tara, you have been alone long enough and have to choose one of these three. Richard and Jack are both cute, and Jake is wealthy too, or give the new john a chance."

I tell her Richard and Jack are wonderful friends to have and keep, and the new John isn't even an option. I am content with everything in my life now, and my soul mate will appear when the time is right for me. Then I ask whether she misses New York or is happy taking these trips.

"Of course, I miss my parents and our friends back home, but nothing can even come close to the vast and awesome experiences of our trips," she says. "I am grateful to you, my best friend, for convincing me. I am making a difference by helping others, meeting new wonderful people, seeing new places, and meeting the love of my life, all thanks to you, Tara, and your angel. And most of all, as you have noticed, I meditate every day and am trying to get Tony to practice it regularly."

Our departure from Nepal is approaching, and we have only one more week left and wish to have everything in order before leaving. We go to the center to discuss the details of our project with Amal one more time and say good-bye to the women who work there. Every time we go there, Rachel gets nervous when she sees the piles of messy paper work and wants to fix them. She was always very neat, and as teenagers, we called her "Miss Organized." So after our talk with Amal, she finally says, "I don't want to intrude, but with your permission, I would like to put all these papers and folders in order, creating an easy system for you to file all the documents."

Amal says they were waiting for someone to take on the task and would be grateful. It takes Rachel and me all day to organize everything and then leave with Richard and Tony.

I say, "Did you really have to do that, Rachel?"

She says, "Yes, or those messy piles of paper would hunt me everywhere."

The next day we go to the market to purchase some souvenirs for our families and friends. The pashmina scarves are soft and colorful, so we each get a few and also some earrings and local crafts. I buy a pashmina and a necklace for my mom and one for Grandma Rita. At night, we call Jack and Bernadette, saying good-bye and hoping to see them soon. Bernadette says we should plan our trip to France for spring, which Rachel and I agree on with pleasure.

We have become friends with Richard's coworkers and are very close with Amal; we would like to see them one more time. So on our last day in Nepal, we go to the women's center again, thanking them for their kindness and hospitality. Hugging Amal, she asks us to take another trip to Kathmandu as soon as we can.

We go to Richard's apartment to celebrate our last night there. Richard opens a bottle of wine, and we all help preparing the food. He is going to supervise Reach's project along with Amal. We talk till past midnight, and none of us want to go to bed, so he opens another bottle of wine, and we talk till almost morning. Then Richard takes us to the airport.

Saying good-bye to him is the hardest, but he promises to visit us in New York and also Arusha if Rachel and I are there.

We are going to Arusha first, and after staying there for few weeks, Rachel and I will depart for New York. Jane is waiting for us at the airport to take us home; she makes tea, and we tell her a little about our trip while drinking our tea. We are expecting Tony to take his bag and go home so the three of us could be alone, but he pours a second tea for himself and isn't leaving. Finally, Rachel kisses him and says, "Now you have to go back home, my love," and practically pushes him out the door.

Tony looks at us with sad eyes, saying, "It was fun being together every day." He kisses

Rachel one more time before leaving. We go to the kitchen and, while preparing food, tell Jane about our trip and things that happened in Nepal. We give her our gifts and some little souvenirs from Nepal. I bought a necklace for her, and Rachel purchased the matching bracelet. We missed each other and don't want to go to bed, but it is two o'clock in the morning. We have much more to talk about and stories to tell Jane but leave those for the next day and, saying good night, go to bed.

In the morning I wake up to the aroma of coffee and go to the kitchen to see Rachel and Jane are preparing breakfast. Jane pours coffee for us, and we sit, enjoying our breakfast. I tell her about meeting Piero, the Italian guy, and describe how humbling it was. After coffee Jane wants us to have an easy day resting and maybe go for a walk. But I am eager to go to the women's center, and so is Rachel. The more help we give, the more connected to everyone and everything I feel, and I want to serve.

Seeing Jane's coworkers is a real joy, and we have a lot of stories from our trip to share with them. So the director of the center suggests that we go to the conference room, where everyone can sit and listen. Rachel and I talk about Amal and Bernadette and their organization's wonderful work in helping women. We tell them about the projects Reach charity is undertaking in Nepal in collaboration with these organizations. And we talk about meeting Piero, the attractive Italian guy. All the younger women take a deep breath, saying, "Ah," wishing they had been there. But then Rachel says, "He is almost ninety years old, and as Amal said, you had to meet him in spirit."

"But I did meet him in spirit, and he is lovely." I explain.

After the meeting, the ladies go back to their work, and Jane asks Rachel and me to talk to a young woman at the center, seeking help. She is a young, beautiful girl name Adina, who starts her story.

"I was just nine years old when my older brother raped me and left me in blood. When I told my parents, they not only didn't punish him but blamed me instead. My father said I had tarnished the family honor, so he found a much older man and gave him some money to marry me. He was lazy and didn't want to work, so he would send me to clean houses for very little money that people would give me. I secretly came to the center and learned to read and write; I also did some handcrafts. I make jewelry and shawls and sell them and have been saving some money. My husband is fifty-five years old, and he sits all day with a bunch of men, smoking. I can't have children because of something that happened to me during the rape. And though I love children, in my situation now, this is a blessing."

"I am seventeen and want to do more in life. I wish to continue school and even go to the university. I would like to become a teacher for children and also help girls and women who are in the same condition. If girls have the same opportunity for education as boys, the number of cases like mine will become less and less."

She continues, "Please, help me get divorced and continue school. If my husband was at least kind and caring, I would stay with him, but he is cruel and keeps calling me damaged and useless."

Rachel and I look at her with empathy; she is intelligent and outspoken. I tell her we will talk to Asha and Jane to see if divorce is possible. Jane says that we will file for divorce, but meanwhile Adina can continue school, and then the center will pay so she can go to the university.

But Adina says, "Please help me get divorced. I can't live with that man anymore."

I truly feel for Adina and want to help her to become free, having the life she wishes for.

In the evening, Tony takes us to Mark's restaurant for dinner. I talk about the fun and productive time we had, with Jack thanking Mark for making the introduction. Gabrielle and Paul join us for dessert and are excited to hear everything regarding our trip and the projects of Reach charity in Nepal. Jane says, "It is time that we have another gathering so all our friends can hear the tales of your travel to Nepal together and see the pictures." Gabrielle says she wants to invite us and is going to call all the other friends.

At night in my prayers, I ask my angel for help to get Adina's divorce. In the middle of the night, I see my angel telling me, "Don't worry, try to help with the divorce procedure, and it will be done sooner than you expect." I wait till the morning to talk to Jane and Rachel about what my angel said.

At work I talk to the center's attorney, encouraging her to start the divorce process right away without hesitation, promising our help in every step. Then we sit with Rachel, preparing all the documents and go with her to file them. When Adina comes to the center and hears the news, she hugs us with tears in her eyes. We have only two more weeks in

Arusha before our return to New York, but I know everything is going to work out. In a few days, the attorney receives the court date. She panics, saying we aren't prepared. And she is scared that Adina's father and husband will become violent. I reassure her and, with Rachel's help, put all the papers in order.

When the day comes, we all go to the court, a little anxious and excited at the same time. The centers attorney does an excellent job presenting her case, and after some argument from the husband's lawyer, the judge rules in Adina's favor, making her divorce official. Outside the court, she jumps up and down, kissing and thanking us over and over. Her father looks at us, saying he will kill her. Asha suggests that Adina live in one of the safe houses while going to school to be protected from her father and brothers. I feel so happy in my heart, thanking my angel.

Tony meets us at Jane's place, and we go to Gabrielle's house together. When we get there, all the other friends have arrived, and they welcome us with some champagne. Gabrielle and Paul's place is similar to Jane's but larger with four bedrooms and more space, and it is decorated modestly with cheerful colors and comfortable but simple furniture. They have prepared a delicious meal with a mix of some

French dishes and some traditional cuisine of Arusha.

We spend a pleasant evening that goes on till dawn, and no one wants to leave. Gabrielle makes some coffee and says, after enjoying the coffee, "You all have to go home." So we do as she says, but saying good-bye isn't easy. They thank Rachel and me for taking this journey and enriching their lives with our friendship. But I say that, on the contrary, it is they who have enhanced our lives and given us many wonderful memories to take home. I am astonished and grateful for the deep connections we have made during our trips, and later Rachel says she feels the same way.

Tony and Rachel take a road trip outside Arusha to be alone and talk. Jane and Gabrielle take the day off, and three of us go to a shopping tour in town. I buy a few more artifacts for my brothers and three beautiful shawls for my mom, Grandma Rita, and Rachel's mom.

At night back in Jane's place, Rachel tells us Tony is sad but understands we have commitments and responsibilities in Nepal and Arusha, and we need more fund-raising. And it is mid-December, and we like to spend Christmas with our family. And Tony's parents insist that he join them for Christmas, so Rachel is happy he isn't going to be alone.

Tony and Jane drive us to the airport. We have decided not to have long and sad good-byes but just to be grateful for the awesome time we had and know we will reconnect soon. We hug and promise to get together in New York or Arusha. Jane says she might come to New York for the holiday.

On the plane, Rachel and I talk about our travels and the impressive people we have met along the way, including the new friends and everything we have accomplished in less than a year. "You can't imagine how thankful and humble I am for God's blessings, Rachel," I say. "It was like wherever we went, someone had gone before us, smoothing the way and arranging everything for our comfort; thus, we could accomplish our mission easily. When we open our hearts and follow our inspiration with service in mind, the universe opens up and provides all the resources and connections needed."

When we arrive at the airport, my Uncle Carlo and Rachel's father are waiting for us. We are tired but excited to see the family; they drive us to Rachel's parents' house. It is eleven o'clock in the morning, and most people are at work, but my mom and Rachel's mom are there, preparing a delicious brunch. They are happy to have us back, saying, "No more long travels, please."

We get some coffee and grab a bite. Then I say, "Let's talk about our travels and future plans another time," asking Uncle Carlo to drive us to my apartment. Rachel says she will go to her place to check things and then repack and come to stay with me. I take a long shower and then sit for meditation, thanking God and my angel for blessing me with the privilege to serve and make a difference in people's lives. I lay on the couch for a little rest but fall asleep and see my angel telling me, "You followed your inspiration, and the universe provided the resources. Go forward with service in mind, and all the blessings and everything you desire will be added."

I wake up from a deep sleep with a knock at the door. It is Rachel, saying she didn't want to be alone and wants to invite me to dinner. "You couldn't stay away from me even for one night," I say, laughing. We catch a cab and go to our favorite Italian restaurant. Seeing Rachel and I, the owner, Ricardo, who is also a friend, comes out, hugging us and asking where we have been and why the long absence. He is right that we haven't been there for almost a year. He gets a table and sits with us, asking, "Now tell me everything from the beginning."

I start telling him about the visions of my angel and our travels and everything that led to the start of Reach Charity. Rachel talks about Tanzania, Nepal, our experiences, and finally the love of her life, Tony. Ricardo looks at us, saying, "You did a lot in less than a year, girls, and are talking about it so nonchalantly, like it's no big deal."

He is upset that we didn't call him on our previous trip for the fund-raising. He wants to participate in our future events and says he is going to donate a percentage of the restaurant's one-night sale to Reach Charity. We spend an extremely pleasant night and, thanking him, leave, happy for yet another source of help.

Rachel says it's time to tell her parents about Tony, but his father might not approve. I say, "You should be honest with them and true to yourself, no matter what happens."

The next day she goes to her parents to tell them about Tony. And I want to spend the day with my mom. I love her dearly, but we haven't always seen eye to eye. My mom isn't even sixty-five; she is young and attractive, but most of the time she is depressed and doesn't have a cheerful attitude. I believe she is still holding on to the hurt from when my father left us. I like to spend some time with her, figuring out a way to help. She worked hard to raise my brothers and me, but we have been independent for many years now.

She has a beautiful apartment, lots of friends, and three successful children who love her. But she doesn't take care of herself, is depressed, and carries her suffering story around like a precious baby. I used to get angry, then scream and yell that she should change her attitude, or I completely avoided seeing her. But since the start of my journey, I have changed my attitude and the way of seeing the world. So twice that we have been back to New York, I feel compassion toward her, trying to spend more time together. Especially this time I see her pain and am determined to help her.

I walk to her apartment, and from there we go to a coffee shop. After some casual talk, she goes back to complaining about her life and being alone and repeating the broken record. I listen patiently for a while but then, taking advantage of a pause, jump in.

"Has being miserable and repeating the same story all these years helped or benefited you in anyway, Mom? So it's time that you change your attitude toward life and think differently. The past has no power over you, Mom. All the potential is in the present moment, and as a perfect child of God, you are capable of doing anything and everything you want. Forgive everyone and anyone that you think has harmed you, and most of all forgive yourself. Forgiveness sets you free, and opens the door to happiness."

I explain how our thoughts become reality, creating our lives. "You manifest in your life anything you imagine and focus on, so stop feeling like a martyr. To change your life, you should change your mind and pay attention to anything you think about, and say."

She looks at me with anguish and suddenly bursts in tears. I can feel her struggle to break through the old habits, but she is afraid. After holding on to a thought for a long time, trying to change it can be frightening, but it isn't hard and just needs willingness and practice.

"I suggest you register in a meditation course and practice it daily and start doing yoga." I tell her we can go together to the meditation center to enroll her and then walk to a restaurant for lunch. "You see, Mom, everything in the world is made of energy vibrating at different frequencies. Sadness and anger have very low energy vibrations, and they consequently keep you at the lowest level of energy. But when you raise your energy to joy and love, you attract the same things to your life."

For the first time, she doesn't argue with me and actually pays attention to what I'm saying. Maybe it's because I have changed and am more tolerant, and she feels my empathy and compassion for her. Our energy and vibration affect other people and our environment, and they respond accordingly.

We walk to the meditation center, where I had taken classes. The instructor welcomes us, asking about my practice; then he puts my mom's name down for a ten-day course in his class. We get lunch at a cozy restaurant close to the meditation center, having a fun and enjoyable time. I ask her to come to Arusha one time and see how other people live. Then we grab a cab to her apartment for tea, and before I leave, she hugs and thanks me for a wonderful day. When we change our minds, thoughts, and the ways we look at things, it is amazing how everything in our lives changes.

I go to my apartment to do some research and make phone calls. When Rachel gets back, we prepare some salad together and have dinner, talking about our days. Rachel says her mom understands she is thirty-four and should do whatever makes her happy. But her father is worried about their financial situation after marriage, and she had to reassure him that they aren't getting married anytime soon or maybe never.

In a few days, we meet with the board and advisory board members at Sara's place to plan another fund-raising event and discuss our projects. Rachel and I talk about Nepal and our two new projects there and the need for much more help. I tell the story of Piero and ask whether we can allocate some small funds for expansion of the school he has built and one of the schools that was damaged during the earthquake. Christmas is approaching, and we are all spending it with our families; therefore, we decide to have a gala for New Year's Eve.

Rachel's parents invite all of us and some friends for Christmas Day, but for Christmas Eve we want to have a small gathering, including my brothers and me, Rachel, and her parents at my mom's place. Since childhood I loved the preparations for Christmas: seeing the lights in streets and stores and when my father decorated our big house, putting lights around it. We would decorate a big tree with lights and ornaments, and the food was a mix of Italian and American traditions for Christmas.

We go with my mom and brothers to choose a tree. I want to take a tall tree, but my mom says it won't fit in the elevator, so we take a smaller one. I am happy to see my mom laughing and looking carefree. She says the meditation sessions have helped her greatly, and they are part of her daily routine now to meditate for twenty minutes every morning. We take the tree to her apartment, and Rachel joins us for decorating it. I put some Christmas music on and take the box of ornaments from the closet; opening it is like revisiting the memories of my childhood. I see with my mind's eye the happy memories and also the not-so-great and rather sad ones. When my dad was home, of course, that ended when I was ten. But the years when Grandma and Grandpa would come to our house and we decorated together were the best days for me.

I jolt out of memory land when Rachel says, "What are you doing Tara? Are we going to decorate or not?"

We decorate the tree with all the old and new ornaments my brothers brought, and then my mom asks me to put the angel on top of the tree. We sit and listen to Christmas music while enjoying some tea with the cake my mom made. Rachel and I go home to do some work and talk to some of our donors.

The next day is decorating the tree at Rachel's parents' place. Her mom has invited us for brunch and decorating. She serves food first and says, "Now get to work." We finish decorating the tree and then put lights and flowers inside the house, and her father decorates the outside with lights. Our moms make the menus for Christmas Eve and day.

Rachel and I go back to my place and call the members of Reach Charity to setup a meeting. We work with other members to send invitations for the New Year's Eve gala. Our friend Sara, the event organizer, is working hard to make this a bigger success than the first one.

My mom is from Sicily Italy and has moved to New York with her parents and brother when she was fourteen. On our Italian side, we have a tradition my Grandma Rita taught us, and she said it has been in her family for generations. The tradition is that the children, instead of asking for different things and gifts at Christmas, write a letter, thanking their parents and God for everything they have in life. They place the letter under the father's plate at Christmas Eve dinner, and he reads it after the food. I don't know whether this was a tradition in all Italian families or just in my grandparents' family. Or Grandma Rita totally invented it to teach her children and grandchildren to show gratitude in life. But whatever was the origin of this tradition, I always loved it and even as a little girl thought that it's better to think of all the good things and blessings in our lives, appreciating them rather than asking for more stuff.

After my father left, my brothers and I put our letters under my mom's plate and continued that routine till we went to college and left home. For years, the tradition was forgotten, but for some reason this year, it has come back to my mind, and so I share it with Rachel and my brothers, and we agree to each write a letter, listing all the blessings in our lives and thanking God for them. Instead of asking for things, we write the ways we can help, no matter how big or small. We tell our parents, and they like the idea. We are going to place our letters in a basket and read them after the Christmas Eve dinner at my mom's. I believe giving gratitude to God and the universe for everything in our lives will open the door to more great possibilities.

Rachel and I go to my mom's apartment in the morning to help making dinner. My mom prepares the Italian seafood dish and puts it in the refrigerator for later when it goes in the oven. Rachel and I wash and cut the vegetables; then my mom says, "Let's take a break for lunch," and she sounds exactly like Grandma Rita.

I say, "We should call Nonna [*Grandma* in Italian] to wish her a Merry Christmas." Nonna picks up the phone and, hearing my voice, screams with joy, saying quietly, "It is my Tara." It is evening in Italy, and her friends are at her place. I talk to her, and then my mom and Rachel talk. She invites the three of us to go there sometimes soon or in March if we want milder weather. I miss her a lot and promise to go for a visit soon. Rachel would be happy going back to Italy, but my mom says she will join us on the next trip.

We set the table, decorate it with flower arrangements, and set out the appetizers. At four o'clock my brothers arrive and then Rachel's parents. We place our letters in a basket and under the tree, then start with appetizers and wine. The traditional Italian dinner goes on for hours. First, we hold hands and pray, giving thanks, then we savor the food, eating slowly and enjoying the conversation. And it comes the time for reading the letters; we each take turns reading our notes. Listening to them makes us feel so connected, as if we are one in our core. They are all incredibly emotional and beautiful; that when it is over, we all have tears in our eyes. My mom says, "It is amazing, when we start counting the blessings in our lives, we realize that they are much more than we had imagined."

The next day Rachel and I go to her parent's house, helping them prepare for another feast.

Christmas is over, and we have to get ready for our New Year's Eve gala. Our friend Sara, is truly working day and night to arrange a gala that as she says, everybody would talk about for months. Help and resources miraculously appear from everywhere. My mom and Rachel's mom help with flower arrangements and the other decorations.

The event goes extremely well, and we raise a large sum of money. I talk about our trip to Nepal and the issues of domestic violence against women and human trafficking. And I finish my speech with a short version of Atal's story—of her capture and then her escape with three other girls. That story brings tears to many eyes and opens their hearts to donate some big sums. A few days after the gala, we get together with other members to discuss our future projects and the potential of expanding to other countries. I say that human trafficking for sex exploitation or forced labor is a huge problem in the world, but many people aren't even aware of it. As the result, it doesn't get enough attention or help to eradicate it. I suggest we distribute more funds to bring awareness to this tragedy facing humanity.

After a few days, Rachel and I go back to Ricardo's restaurant to thank him for all the help he provided for the gala. He welcomes us as usual with a big smile and compliments us on the huge popularity of the event.

Rachel and I brainstorm for choosing our base, where we would rather live most of the time. I ask her whether she prefers living in Arusha or here in New York. She says, "Why don't we choose the next country for expansion of Reach, go there, and then come back home, since our families are here and we have our apartments?"

I think it's a great idea, but for now we can travel to different countries as long as our finances allow and then settle down somewhere. "I know you miss Tony, but before going back to Arusha, we can visit Nonna Rita since she has invited us."

"Tony is still in England for the holiday so we can enjoy a vacation in Italy," Rachel says.

I ask my mom to join us, but she wants to continue the meditation course and is volunteering at a homeless shelter. I am content and amazed at the huge change in her outlook on life and the difference it has made; she even looks much younger.

Part 4

ITALY

No other Force comes close
to the power of love.

Rachel calls Tony in England, telling him we are going to visit Grandma Rita in Italy. Toward the end of January, Rachel and I are on our way to Rome. We arrive at the airport in the morning, and after getting our luggage, we grab a cab and go to the hotel, Ricardo suggested. It is a clean and moderately priced hotel close to Via Veneto. We go to our room and, after taking a shower, get out for coffee and breakfast.

The weather is cold, so we button our coats and walk fast, entering the first coffee shop on the way. We sit at the table and order cappuccino and some pastries. I am so glad my grandma insisted that we learn Italian, since some people don't speak English at all or maybe only a little. The waiter doesn't speak English very well and gives us an unfriendly look, but when I start speaking Italian fluently with a perfect accent, he changes his attitude and becomes too friendly, standing next to our table and talking till his boss calls him. We want to stay in Rome for a week and then continue our trip.

Rome, the capital of Italy, is a metropolitan city with a rich history you can feel just by walking its streets. You see glory of art everywhere: the statues, the elaborate fountains, and the mastery used in making them. We walk on Via Veneto, that is one of the most famous, elegant, and expensive streets of Rome with many café and restaurants. It is home to famous designer boutiques with extremely high prices. Via Veneto, is close to Spanish Steeps that is one of the major tourist attractions in Rome.

"Imagine how much work we can do in Nepal with five thousand dollars, the price of just one bag," Rachel says, "and that isn't even expensive for some people." It is great to earn a lot of money and manifest wealth in your life, but it's definitely a wonderful idea to give some for helping the less fortunate people. And I think it's our human duty to care for and help one another.

I called my cousin Roberto from New York, letting him know we would be in Rome, so we walk back to the hotel, where he is going to meet us around noon. And he is already there, waiting for us. He has a mini car, the kind most people have in major cities of Europe. Rachel and I are both tall girls and have to bend to get into the car. Roberto wants to take us to Tivoli Gardens, which is outside Rome; on our last trip, we didn't get to visit the place.

He drives extremely fast, but that is how most people drive around here. The Villa d'Este is a sixteenth-century villa in Tivoli, near Rome; it is famous for its terraced hillside Italian Renaissance garden, especially for the large number of magnificent fountains. It is now an Italian State Museum and is listed as a UNESCO World Heritage Site. We get out of the car, shaking ourselves, straightening our bodies, and walk toward the museum first. The garden and fountains in all different shapes and sizes are absolutely splendid.

We walk for hours, enjoying the beauty and artistry used to create this garden. Roberto takes us to our hotel to get some rest and get ready for dinner, and we are invited to his sister's house. Roberto comes back around seven to drive us to my cousin Clara's place; she is in her fifties and lost her husband five years ago. It is about a thirty minutes' drive away, so it's not bad with Roberto's driving.

Clara is warm and very hospitable. She has prepared a feast, starting with a glass of Marsala wine and appetizers such as roasted tomato with goat cheese bruschetta, spinach and mozzarella cheese bruschetta, and other varieties. Clara is a fun-loving person who always has a positive attitude and appreciates her blessings in life. After losing her husband five years ago due to a terrible car accident, she was left alone with two teenage girls, but she never complains or says anything negative. And it is for this reason that people get attracted to her, and she has many friends. She has invited some of them.

After a few glasses of wine and an appetizer, she takes Rachel and me to the kitchen, saying that her friends are among wealthy and influential people; she wants us to talk about Reach Charity and our travels. She says we are going to have fun enjoying our evening and at the same time trying to get some donation for your projects. Then she gives each of us a dish to put on the dinner table, saying, "Tara and Rachel are guests of honor, and I am making them work."

In Italian gatherings dinner usually takes two hours or more with eating, drinking, and having conversation. After dinner Roberto makes espresso; Clara brings the desserts and asks Rachel and me to talk about our charity organization and the need for help. I speak about our trips and the emotional experiences that led us to start Reach Charity. Rachel tells them the story of the Italian guy in Nepal, and all Clara's friends listen with interest. It is almost morning when Clara's friends leave and Roberto drives us to the hotel.

In the morning after our meditation, we want to go out for cappuccino and breakfast. But, exiting from the elevator, we see Clara waiting for us at the lobby. She has been waiting for thirty minutes, thinking we might be asleep. She wants us to grab our bags and go stay with her for the rest of our time in Rome. Clara says we shouldn't pay for the hotel when she has two extra rooms with bathrooms, since her daughters are in college. The arrangement makes sense, so we inform the hotel and leave for the coffee shop.

After ordering our coffee, Clara gives me an envelope full of checks and says she has some donations from her friends for Reach Charity projects in Nepal. It is wonderful, unexpected news that makes Rachel and me scream with joy, causing everyone at the coffee shop to give us a strange look, probably thinking, *Ah, these Americans.*

We walk to the post office to mail the checks to the organization's accountant and then go to the hotel to pick up our bags. Clara dedicates all her time to Rachel and me, taking us sight-seeing or shopping or mostly window-shopping. And every night we are invited to dinner at one of her friends' place. We had planned to visit Florence, but Clara and her friends insist that Rachel and I stay in Rome. They all want to invite us, but there isn't enough time. We are super comfortable with Clara and have a great time with her friends, but it is time to continue our trip to Marsala.

Marsala is an elegant, historic town located in the province of Trapani in the westernmost part of Sicily and is famous for its wine, baroque-era buildings, and quaint shops. Marsala is also known for being the landing place for Garibaldi and his thousands of men on May 11, 1860; that started the chain of events before Italy's unification. Giuseppe Garibaldi was an Italian general, politician and nationalist who played a large role in the history of Italy.

Throughout the town, you can see commemorative plaques, pictures of Garibaldi, and a variety of businesses that have chosen the name Garibaldi.

When we arrive at Trapani's airport, a driver is waiting to take us to Grandma Rita's villa. Coming to Marsala, my ancestral home where my mom was born, always gives me a warm feeling. I think that next time, taking a trip here will be with my mom. Nonna Rita hugs me tightly and starts crying. "Don't worry, baby. Grandma will find a perfect man for you."

"I am fine and happier, Nonna—no need for a man. Wait till you hear about our amazing year."

She then hugs Rachel, "Thanks for being such a good friend to my Tara."

"But she has been the best friend for me, Nonna, and has led me to many adventures that have enriched my life in so many ways," Rachel answers. The maid serves some wine and an appetizer, but Nonna says, "Don't fill yourself. We have prepared a feast for your arrival."

I tell her about our trips and the sad stories we had heard; we also talk about the incredible people who proved the power of the human mind and spirit to us. She likes the name Reach Charity, saying that it fits our work and encourages us to continue going forward and always to have faith, asking God for guidance. She continues, "Going through life, the older you get, the more you realize that all that matters in life is love, kindness, and sharing your fortune with others. With the energy of love, we can connect to the entire universe—moon, sun, stars—and even reach to heaven."

"Wow, Nonna, I didn't know this spiritual side of you," I say.

She says, "I was introduced to meditation when you were not born yet and have been meditating every day for one hour or sometimes more. And I always served people in need in any way that was possible for me, and sometimes they didn't know where the help had come from."

We sit and enjoy the delicious food, listening to Grandma's stories. After dinner she says, "The house servant will show you to your bedrooms."

But Rachel says, "No, thank you, Nonna. One room is fine."

"Rachel can't be away from me, Nonna," I say, laughing.

She says, "However it is more comfortable. Now I am going to bed. We will talk more tomorrow, but you can stay and have dessert and wine or watch TV."

We stay, talking for hours and drinking Marsala wine, which I am beginning to like.

Rachel says, "It feels great to be pampered like this sometimes, having money and just traveling to help."

"If that is what you really want, set the intention, send it to the universe, and believe in it. But the wealth has to be used for helping people and advancing our planet collectively." I say.

"I work on it, putting the request to the universe, but for now let's be grateful for this luxury and being taking care of," Rachel replies.

In the morning Grandma's maid serves us two cups of coffee in our room, saying Grandma is waiting for us at the breakfast table. Taking a deep breath, Rachel says, "Oh, I love you, the universe."

We join Grandma and enjoy our breakfast. She asks about my mom, saying, "How is my beautiful little girl, Alegra? Why doesn't she come here? It is her house, and I keep inviting her."

I explain that my mom has changed her attitude and the way she views the world, and that has affected her life dramatically. And now she meditates, and is happier, healthier, and joyful.

"Thank God for that. You know, Tara, your mom was always a drama queen. She loved to be miserable, though she grew up in a loving and comfortable house but created a sad story for herself out of every little thing, and was attached to it. I had to explain to her many times that we create our own universe inside us. There is a Field of Absolute Blessings in the world I call FAB, which interestingly is short for 'fabulous.' And there is also a Field of Absolute Suffering or Shit, which I call FAS. It is our choice to draw and attract things we desire from FAB or FAS. We are free to decide if we want to live in a friendly universe or a hostile one. I explained this to your mom many times, but she wasn't willing to change. This is a wonderful news you finally were able to make her understand to get out of her self-pity, realizing that the universe is friendly." Says Grandma Rita.

"I love this analogy. Why hadn't you told us this before, Nonna?" Rachel says, laughing. "We have to be careful, always staying in FAB and never going even near FAS."

I promise Nonna that next time we will visit her with my mom. She asks about our experiences and likes to hear the stories of our adventures. I tell her about the extraordinary people we have met, such as Susan, Bernadette and Piero.

Then I say, "I admire Piero, who gave up his life of luxury and comfort, dedicating himself solely to helping others, and has found incredible joy in that. I have chosen the path of service to reach out and help as many as possible that is within my power. Helping others makes me more than happy, and is my life purpose, but I enjoy luxury and would like comfort and pleasure in my own life, too. And I believe that is entirely feasible, and as a matter of fact, it is our birthright."

"Double that, my friend. I totally agree," Rachel says.

"If that is what you want, hold the intention, send it to the FAB (Field of Absolute Blessings), and every day do your part, and the universe will provide the rest for you," Grandma says.

After breakfast she has some business to attend but has arranged for a car to take us sight-seeing. The driver, an extremely polite guy, a native of Marsala, opens the car door for us with a friendly smile, asking where we would like to go. We would like to visit the town historic center and the cathedral, and we walk to look at the shops.

In the evening we go back to be with Grandma. As we are having some wine and talking, she says, "I had put some money aside to give you for a wedding gift, but now it is yours to use for the travel expenses, and I also would like to donate a check for Reach Charity."

I hug her, saying, "That is exactly what I had asked FAB (Field of Absolute Blessings): to travel with peace of mind, not worrying about money."

We sit for dinner and of course Marsala wine; who dares to bring the name of another wine?

Rachel whispers in my ear, "If we can have some chianti," but seeing my shock from the question, she raises her glass of Marsala wine, thanking Grandma for her hospitality and kindness. After a few days, Grandma says she wants to invite some of her friends for a gathering on our honor. She wants us to talk about the organization and our projects, saying that some of the guests might be interested in getting involved.

"Who are these friends, Nonna?" I say. "We travel very light and don't have any party dress."

"Don't worry. They aren't all old like your Nonna. And I have spoken to a friend of mine, who owns an exclusive boutique for cocktail dresses. You and Rachel should go and select what you like; she will send me the bill later."

Rachel wants to pay for her own, but Grandma says, "Don't be silly. You are like my granddaughter too, and it is just a small gift."

The driver is ready to take us to the boutique. The owner welcomes us, saying that Grandma is a dear friend of hers. We each try on a few dresses, and I choose a light-green dress that enhances the green in my eyes. And Rachel selects a dark-blue one with an open back, saying that she wishes Tony was here to see her.

But she is in for a surprise. Knowing how much she misses Tony, I called him in England, where he still is, and asked that he join us on the night of Grandma's party. We go home happy, like two kids on Christmas morning, opening their gifts. Grandma Rita approves our choices of dress, saying that before the gathering that is in two days, we should go to a hairdresser. I explain to her that Rachel and

I prefer a more natural look; she insists for a while but finally accepts.

At night sitting for meditation, I feel loneliness in my heart. In my prayers, I say it's time for meeting the perfect man and put this thought into the universe. And before falling sleep, I ask my angel to bring the right man for me into my life. In the middle of the night, I see my angel, saying, "It was about time to ask. Trust God, and you will soon meet your soul mate."

I wake up with a smile on my face, thinking, *An angel with a sense of humor.*

On the day of the gathering, Rachel and I help making the flower arrangements to place around the house and a large one for the dinner table centerpiece. I know Tony will arrive in the evening. I am supposed to keep Rachel in our room while the maid is taking Tony to one of the guest rooms to get ready. When we are ready and go to the salon, I will tell the maid to get Tony.

Around seven o'clock, the guests start arriving: first a young couple who are distant relatives and then a lady in her sixties, a widow called Sofia who is Grandma's neighbor. Then other guests arrive; some are Grandma's age, but most are younger, even as young as

Rachel and I. Grandma introduces us to her friends and gives me an inquiring look, and suddenly, I think, *Oh my God. Tony is waiting in the room for our signal to make a grand entrance.* I run and tell the maid to get him and then start a conversation with Rachel so she won't see Tony as he enters the room.

He quietly comes behind Rachel and taps on her shoulder; she turns to see who it is. Then she starts screaming and jumping in his arms. She keeps looking at Tony and screaming; the guests are puzzled about what has happened. Finally, Grandma, holding her, says, "Rachel dear, you and Tony go to the other room and do your kissing, shouting, and other stuff. Then come back."

Laughing, Rachel says, "Sorry, Grandma, but what is he doing here? And we don't have any stuff." But Grandma pushes them out and comes back to me.

We walk around, and she introduces me to all her friends with big pride. I notice that she keeps looking at the door and then at her watch. I ask, "Are you waiting for someone, Nonna?"

She says, "The food is ready, and all the guests are here but one. The servants are waiting for my signal to start setting the food on the table."

I say, "Who is this rude guest? Why should everyone wait for one person? Let's just serve the dinner." I haven't finish my sentence when the doorbell rings, and with that my life changes forever.

One of the servants opens the door, and I see a tall, handsome guy entering the room. He has a wide smile, showing his perfectly straight, white teeth. Grandma greets him warmly and, taking his arm, walks toward me. She introduces him as Dr. Lorenzo and leaves us. He shakes my hand and holds it for few minutes, and that feels like much longer to me. He says, "I am Lorenzo." I gently pull my hand away, introducing myself.

He says, "I recognized you from the beautiful photos Grandma has shown us, but you are much more beautiful in person." For some reason, I feel nervous but try to look calm, thinking, *Please don't blush. Please don't blush.*

He holds my arm as if we have been friends forever and, walking, says, "Grandma is very proud of you and talks about your great work all the time. Can you tell me about your projects?"

I look for Rachel to come and rescue me, but she is busy with Tony, not paying attention to anybody else. "I have to help Grandma with dinner," I say, "but later we will talk more."

I go looking for Rachel and Tony, who are still in each other's arms, kissing.

"That is enough," I say. "You will have time later. They are serving dinner, and I have to talk to you, Rachel."

She jumps up, kissing me and saying, "You are the best friend. Thanks for asking Tony to come here."

We join the rest of the guests at the table. Raising her glass of wine, Grandma says, "My dear friends, thank you for joining here in honor of my Tara and her friend Rachel, who is part of our family too."

They all raise their glasses, and Rachel and I thank everyone. Then plenty of delicious food and wine is consumed. And there are a lot of loud conversations in Italian; it seems everyone is talking at the same time, and no one is listening. I'm glad Tony is here to talk to Rachel, or she would be lost in this all-Italian, noisy crowd. She understands some Italian, but not when the conversation goes so fast. We go to the other room for dessert and espresso, or tea.

Lorenzo sits next to me, and we talk about everything: our lives, work, and goals and dreams for the future. Then Grandma calls me and Rachel to speak about our experiences in Tanzania and Nepal, which led to the start of Reach Charity. They all listen attentively and show interest to get involved and help.

Then the guests are leaving, thanking Grandma and us, but Lorenzo clearly has no desire to go home. Finally, Grandma says she is tired and wants to go to her room. Looking at Lorenzo, she adds, "You stay, dear, as long as the girls and Tony are up."

The four of us sit and talk till almost morning, and then Lorenzo leaves to get a few hours of sleep before going to the hospital. Grandma has kindly invited Tony to stay in one of the guest rooms.

When we go to our room, Rachel says, "It seems that your soul mate has arrived, Tara. You two were talking all night, not paying attention to anyone else. What was he saying?"

"You were busy with Tony yourself, and didn't see that I conversed with all the guests. And we were talking about our work; he is a cardiologist, a native of Marsala, and his family and my grandparents have been friends for many years. What attracted me is that every year he travels for three months with a group of doctors to different countries, performing free heart surgery for people in need. And if there are no hospitals, they fly them to the nearest city."

"And that is the *only* factor for your attraction?" Rachel says jokingly.

In the morning we sleep in, and after we shower, we go down for breakfast. Tony and Nonna are drinking their coffee, having an apparently interesting conversation since none of them notice us. When we say good morning, Grandma says, "My girls, did you enjoy the gathering last night? We were talking about safaris with Tony. I had been to one as a young girl but would like to come to Tanzania one time and take another safari with you."

We haven't finished our breakfast when Lorenzo calls, saying that he is taking advantage of the few minutes' free time before his next patient. He is calling to talk to me and wants to invite us for dinner. I say we will call him later with the answer. Grandma says she can't party two nights in a row, but we should accept. I don't want to leave her alone, but she insists that we go, saying she likes to relax.

I talk to Lorenzo, and he is going to pick us up at seven o'clock in the evening. We spend the rest of the day with Grandma, talking and putting the rooms back in order after the big gathering. She tells us Lorenzo's parents own one of the biggest wineries in the countryside of Marsala and wanted him to continue in the family business, but he was interested in medicine instead and wanted to become a doctor. She wants to know my opinion of Lorenzo and whether I like him. But before I can give any answer, Rachel says, "Yes, Nonna, she does."

Grandma, with her usual sense of humor, says, "How did you notice, dear, being all occupied with Tony?"

Sofia, Grandma's neighbor, calls, inviting us for coffee the next morning at eleven o'clock in the morning.

At seven Lorenzo arrives and comes inside to thank Grandma first, but before we leave, she asks him to take us one day for a tour of their winery. We go to a cozy restaurant in the center of the town, which Lorenzo says is known for traditional homemade-style cuisine. The owner hugs Lorenzo and welcomes us, saying our table is ready. We spend a fun night, eating and drinking; then Lorenzo wants to take us to a café that is famous for the best desserts and espresso. It is a quaint café, beautifully decorated with colorful Italian ceramics. Lorenzo asks us what kind of dessert we like, saying, "They make the best of all Italian desserts."

We order espresso with cannoli and crostata, which is an open-faced fruit tart. We like all Italian desserts but wouldn't want to gain weight now. I take a bite of the cannoli, but this is so delicious that justifies a few extra pound. We talk till past midnight. Lorenzo is very interested in our projects and wants to help us expand to other countries. He has been to Nepal and is aware of the issue of trafficking the young girls and women. He says it is a sad problem facing humanity, and we should all help in any way possible to eradicate it.

It is after midnight, and the owner wants to close. He says, "Lorenzo, my wife likes you, but if I go home any later than this, even your name will not stop her from killing me."

We all laugh and leave, thanking him. When we get home, Lorenzo kisses me on the cheek, saying he will call the next day. Tony opens the door with the key Grandma gave us. We enter quietly, and each goes to his or her room, since Grandma and her servant are asleep.

Rachel says, "True love has finally found you, my friend."

"He is a wonderful man, but we just met, and I am not sure yet." In bed I pray, saying, "Thank you, my angel, for answering my request, but I didn't expect it to happen this quickly."

I see my angel in a dream, saying, "Your heart is pure and open. Don't close it to love. Trust yourself, and know it is safe to love again. I listened to your prayers and sent them to heaven, but truly it is you who manifested your desire by raising your energy vibration to the level of love. You asked for a soul mate and can't send it back now." Waking up, I think definitely an angel with a sense of humor is with me, and I love it.

In the morning Rachel, seeing my cheerful attitude, says, "What were you dreaming last night?"

"I decided to be open to the potential of love and not worry about it." Then I tell her what my angel said.

"I love your angel, Tara. She is very cool."

Grandma looks at me joyfully, giving the impression that she knows everything.

We are invited to Sofia's house, but Tony doesn't want to join us, saying it is a women's gathering, and that he wouldn't feel comfortable. Grandma says she has some work to do and likes Tony to stay with her. Rachel and I walk to the next-door villa, and as we get close to the gate, it opens, and a voice says, "Welcome. Please come in."

We walk on a road surrounded by tall trees that open up to a beautiful, round garden with pink and purple flowers. A few short stairs lead to a wide balcony with ornate wrought-iron fences. Sofia comes down the stairs, hugging us warmly and showing us to the sunroom. She is in her sixties with a vibrant and energetic personality. She says her husband passed away a few years ago after a long sickness, and she has one son who lives in Rome with his family. She continues, saying that losing her loving husband was extremely hard on her. But self-pity and feeling sorry for herself weren't an option, so she decided to do something positive with her life. She went back to school and got her degree in education; and now she teaches as a volunteer at schools in low-income neighborhoods.

The maid serves cappuccino and homemade cake, and as we are enjoying them, Sofia asks about Reach Charity and its projects. I tell her the story; in short. She is very interested in becoming part of it and helping. Sofia says she would love to travel to these places, visiting the girls, but it might be too late for her.

"It is never too late to try something new or to do the things you always wanted to do, but life got in the way, and it was forgotten," I say.

"That is true. Maybe one time we can travel together to Nepal and other countries."

We have been talking for hours, not noticing the time. Grandma and Tony are waiting for us, so we have to leave. She invites us to go back with Nonna and Tony.

"We can discuss our projects then and will certainly use your help in the future," Rachel says. We get Tony and go for a long walk. Rachel and Tony ask me about Lorenzo and our relationship.

"I don't know," I say. "We met just two days ago, but anything is possible."

At home Nonna tells me Lorenzo has called to talk to me. He wants to invite me out for dinner, saying, "Alone if possible, just the two of us." But I'd rather spend the night at home with Nonna, so we postpone that event for the next evening. We have only one more week in Marsala, and I would like to spend it more with my grandma. We sit with Grandma, having some wine and an appetizer; it seems that she really likes Tony, so four of us spend a fun and relaxed evening. After dinner we take Nonna for a short walk, and then she goes to her room, saying we can order anything we want before that the maid retires for the night.

But I go to our room to sit for meditation, leaving Rachel and Tony to be alone. I sit for a long meditation and then ask for guidance of how to continue doing my passion and purpose, traveling to different countries now that Lorenzo is in my life. My angel comes to me, saying, "Follow your heart, Tara. You can continue doing what you love and have Lorenzo. Have faith in your ability and tell Rachel she has a cool angel, too, and she can call her whenever she wants."

Everyone has an angel and can communicate with the angel if he or she choose to. In the morning, I tell Rachel about what my angel said. She gets excited, saying, "Cool. I will speak with her tonight."

At breakfast I say, "Lorenzo has invited me to dinner alone," and I ask what Nonna thinks about it. She says I should accept the invitation and that he is a wonderful gentleman. Then she hugs me, saying how happy this makes her, knowing that Lorenzo and I are perfect together.

"How do you know, Nonna?"

"I knew it even before your trip here that the two of you are totally compatible and well matched." We go out to lunch with Nonna and Sofia, who has a loving energy that makes you want to be with her. In the evening, I ask Rachel and Tony to join us for dinner, but she refuses, saying, "First of all, Tony and I like to go out and have the evening to ourselves. And imagine how it will look if, when Lorenzo comes to pick you up, Tony and I appear and jump in the car. You don't need a chaperone, Tara. Go and have fun."

Nonna says, "Yes, Tara, listen to your friend and tell me everything tomorrow at breakfast." We go to our room to get ready.

Rachel says, "You were never timid, Tara. Even as a little girl, I remember you always getting in trouble for your outspoken tongue. What is different about this guy that makes you nervous?"

"I don't know, but am happy to go out with him and discover!"

In the evening, Lorenzo arrives at six o'clock. We kiss Nonna, and the four of us go out the door together, just to see how he reacts. Seeing Rachel and Tony with me, Lorenzo looks utterly disappointed. But, trying to be polite, he says, "It is great that you are joining us, too."

Laughing, Rachel says, "Don't panic, Lorenzo. We have our own plans." They have called a taxi, so Lorenzo and I leave in his car. He drives to a restaurant by the water with fantastic view. Lorenzo gives his name, and the hostess leads us to our table. And as we sit, the owner, who is Lorenzo's friend, welcomes us warmly and orders a bottle of wine. Suddenly, I feel comfortable and at ease.

We eat, drink, and talk till after midnight. I find out we have a lot in common, sharing the same passion for helping and making a difference in the world. Then Lorenzo talks about his love, saying that from the first moment he lay eyes on me, he knew I was the love of his life. He bends over the table, kissing me. He says, "I know you want to travel and help, so we have to make it work. We can see each other as many times as possible in the year, since for now my work is here."

I think, as Grandma said, that we truly are compatible. It is past midnight, and we have to go back, but none of us is ready. When we get to Grandma's house, he kisses me on the lips, and I kiss him back to show my feelings are mutual. Rachel and Tony are back and waiting for me in the family room. They ask about our dinner and what we did.

"We did a lot," I say, "and I can't tell you all of it."

Tony hugs me, saying, "It was about time," and goes to his room.

Rachel wants to know if we kissed. I say, "Yes, and it was delicious but not a long French kiss like you and Tony."

She says, "Wait a few days, and you will get there."

We have only five more days, but Grandma insists that we extend our stay, saying this might be the last time to see her. "What are you saying? What about taking a safari, and next time we will come for a visit with my mom? Don't you want to see your daughter?"

"That is my greatest wish to have some time with you and your mom, so I have to stick around for now."

"Rachel and I will talk and decide to stay one more week, since in Nepal Amal and Bernadette are overseeing our projects, and in Tanzania we have Jane. I would like to have more time with Lorenzo and get to know him better."

We have about two more weeks in Marsala and want to make the most of them. Our days are spent with Grandma, and most of the time Sofia joins us. Some days Rachel and Tony go out together, and I stay with my grandma. We have become close friends with Sofia, and she definitely wants to be part of Reach Charity. She has a lot of wealthy friends and wants to organize some fund-raising event at her villa. For dinners usually Lorenzo and I go out together, and Tony and Rachel go separately, but some nights the four of us go together. Grandma loves Lorenzo, saying he is like her grandson and enjoys his company when he joins us for dinner at home.

Now I feel totally comfortable with Lorenzo, thinking Grandma is right. We are truly compatible in every way. His mission is to help, and he loves traveling to different parts of the world, doing heart surgery for people who are in critical condition but can't afford to pay for the operation. He has one brother, who is a few years older, is married, and has one daughter. He tells me that his parents wanted him and his brother to take over the winery so they could retire. But Lorenzo had a different passion, and his parents tried to persuade him to join his brother, but in the end they respected his decision. We talk about our future and decide to have faith and trust our love for one another. He says after three months, he is going to take some time off work and will join me wherever I am, and we can spend some time together.

During our last weekend in Marsala, Lorenzo's parents have invited us to their winery for a small gathering with a few of their friends. Lorenzo and his brother, Fabio, have brought their cars to take us to the winery. Grandma and I go with Lorenzo; and Rachel, Tony, and Sofia go with Fabio.

It is about an hour's drive in beautiful, green countryside. During the drive grandma gives Lorenzo and me some words of advice. "Always love and respect one another, but at the same time give each other some space and let your unique self shine. We are all divine beings with our special gift, and each has a purpose in life that he or she has to fulfill. Walk and work together through life, but let the breeze of heaven dance between you."

I love what she says; it absolutely fits my personality.

When we get to the winery, Lorenzo's parents, Fabio's wife, and some other family members walk to the car to welcome us. And they all are curious to meet me. After the usual introduction, we go inside the large salon, which has a wine bar and a long table next to it at one side, and different furniture settings across the room. The room is decorated with colorful flowers, and appetizers are set on the long table.

Lorenzo's parents are friendly and warm, putting me at ease immediately. They pour some wine and ask us to gather around the appetizer table. Lorenzo's father raises his glass.

"Tara, I am honored to welcome you to our family with love and an open heart. My son is so involved with his work and travels that we had lost hope of him ever falling in love until you came along and in this short time changed everything. For this I am grateful and hope he deserves your love."

He speaks with such love and sincerity that he brings tears to my eyes. I hug and kiss him and Lorenzo's mom. We sit in small groups around each table, drinking wine and having antipasto, which is the Italian word for an appetizer. Lorenzo's mom tells me that our families have been close friends for generations. She was my mom's childhood friend, and they were going to the same school until my grandparents left for New York.

After the wine tasting, we go to the basement, where the wine is made, and then to the cellar, where they keep the wine. The winery is an old, beautiful building surrounded by acres of vineyards, and we enjoy walking through the land. We spend a lovely day, and when saying good-bye, I promise to come back for another visit with my mom soon.

For our last few days in Marsala, we decide to spend it all together. During the days, Rachel and I are with Grandma and Sofia. Tony stays home, reading, or goes out for a walk, and for dinner Lorenzo joins us at home. I enjoy spending time with my Nonna and don't want to leave her, but Lorenzo wants to have some alone time with me too.

For our final day in Marsala, Lorenzo takes off from work, so we go out together. Tony and Rachel will spend time alone, and at night we all join at home to be with Grandma and Sofia. Lorenzo drives to a restaurant by the water, and we sit, talking for hours. He doesn't want to lose me, and kissing my hands over and over, he says how much I mean to him. It is evening, and we have promised Grandma to be home.

When we get home, Tony, Rachel, and Sofia are there. We stay till midnight, and Grandma sits with us, telling stories about old times and about Grandpa and when my mom and Uncle Carlo were kids. She says my mom always acted like a princess, and Grandpa called her "my *principessa*" in Italian.

It is past midnight, and Grandma is tired and wants to go to her room. Saying good night, I ask Lorenzo and Sofia to watch over my grandma. But she laughs and says, "It is the other way around, so don't worry, Tara. I take care of them."

The next day Lorenzo comes to drive us to the airport. We don't like to say good-bye, so we just hug and say, "See you soon" to Grandma and Sofia, who walked here early to be with us. At the airport, Lorenzo holds me for a long time, saying he doesn't want to let me go.

I say, "Believe that we are going to be together soon." We have a long, hot kiss, and I gently pull myself away. Tony is going back to England, but he and Rachel are used to this separating and reconnecting again, but for Lorenzo and me, it is the first time.

On the plane, Rachel says she really likes Lorenzo and thinks he is the one. Meeting Lorenzo on this trip was completely unexpected, but I am happy it happened, though I asked my angel but didn't presume it would come true this fast. We haven't told anyone about the day and time of our return.

After getting our luggage, we grab a cab and go to my apartment. After taking our showers and getting some rest, we go out to buy some groceries. "Let's call our parents tomorrow and tonight we do some work and try to decide our next country and then discuss it with other board members. With the big check my grandma gave me, we can travel for a while. That is for our travel expenses."

"What do I do?" Rachel says.

I hug her saying don't worry Rachel, "I can pay for your ticket, and the rest God will provide."

"Remember, your thoughts become reality, Rachel. Don't think of the lack or obstacles or other things you don't want. Focus on what you want, visualize it clearly, and raise your energy vibration to love, joy, and, most of all, gratitude. Believe you already have it in your life, and be grateful for it. Remember that you have an angel, too, and can talk and communicate with her, asking for guidance."

"I did see my angel and talked to her when we were in Italy, and it was awesome, but I forgot to tell you about it," Rachel says.

"How could you forget something this important? Now ask about our next destination."

In the morning, Rachel goes to her parents' house, and I call my mom. She is on her way to meditation class and says we can meet for lunch at our usual café. I go for a run and then get ready and walk to the café. I get a table and sit after about ten minutes. My mom arrives, and seeing her, I can't believe my eyes due to the huge transformation.

She has lost some weight and looks younger and energetic, and is radiating joy and self-confidence. She hugs and kisses me with so much love I hadn't felt from her in a long time. For years we just exchanged a cold, mechanical hug. It is amazing how changing your thoughts, attitudes, and energy transforms everything in your life. I am so glad to see her happy and positive. She tells me I was right, and now every day, counting her blessings, she gives thanks to the universe. She meditates regularly and does volunteer work in a homeless shelter.

She says, "You were right, Tara. Changing my thoughts and energy made a world of difference in my life, and I even met a wonderful man in the yoga class."

I say jokingly, "Wow, Mom, did you say twice that Tara is right? Could you please write that down first and then tell me everything about this new man?"

She says, "He is a retired businessman who made a fortune from his company. He has been divorced for many years and has one son who is running their business now. He is a kind and generous man, and we have fun together."

She asks about Grandma Rita and my trip to Marsala. I hesitate a little but then tell her everything concerning Lorenzo and our relationship. She is surprised and happy, saying it was about time I gave love another chance.

We spend an enjoyable time without getting into an argument. She says her boyfriend, Tom, would like to meet me and know everything regarding our charity. I say, "We will talk about that and set a time for our meeting."

I buy some groceries, go home, and call the other board members to talk and get updates. In the evening, Rachel comes home, and we make dinner together.

"Did you talk to your angel?" I ask her.

"Yes, and it was the best experience. I asked about our next step, and she said, 'Go back to Tanzania and continue your work. The universe will clear the path ahead.' I think it is a great idea, and from there we can decide. We can stay about two weeks in New York and then leave for Arusha. I miss Jane and our friends in Arusha, and it would be wonderful to see them."

Our days in New York are divided between going to work and spending time with our family and friends. After a few days, my mom's boyfriend, Tom, invites Rachel and me to dinner. We meet at seven o'clock in the evening at the restaurant where he has reservations.

When Rachel and I arrive at the restaurant my mom, and Tom are already there. They are sitting at the table, holding hands. Tom welcomes us and pulls out chairs for us to sit. He is in his late sixties and looks fit and energetic, and he looks younger than his age. He has traveled all around the world and speaks different languages; interestingly, Italian is one of those.

Tom orders a bottle of champagne. "My Allegra likes this, but if you prefer something else, please tell me."

He is interested in hearing about our work and the future plans for expanding our reach. I tell him a little about our travels and what led us to start our organization, Reach. Rachel recounts some of the stories we have heard or seen firsthand. Tom says human trafficking is a colossal issue facing humanity now, and that we all should join hands and efforts to eradicate it and help the victims. He wants to donate some funds for building a safe house and an educational center in Nepal. My mom says she and Tom would like to go for a visit to Nepal with us.

We have a fun, long dinner and interesting conversations till the waiter tells us they want to close the restaurant. Tom and my mom take us to my apartment and leave.

"I like him; he is intelligent, cultural, and kind—and he wants to help," Rachel says. "Isn't it amazing? Whoever we meet offers to donate money and give us a helping hand."

"See, Rachel, we plant a seed, and it grows and spreads like the butterfly effect. That is how the universe provides all the resources when we trust God and ask with pure hearts for the benefit of all humanity."

Lorenzo calls almost every morning when it is their night and when he is back from work, and we talk as long as I have time. He tells me how much he loves and misses me. And I miss him too, but for now we are going to Tanzania, and his work is in Italy. Tony is back in Arusha, and Rachel is happy to see him soon. This time my mom and Tom take us to the airport, saying that on the next trip, we will all go together.

Jane and Tony are at the airport to take us home. At Jane's place Tony sits with us for an hour and then leaves, saying, "I know you have a lot to talk about, especially Tara."

It feels warm and comfortable being back with Jane. She puts some snacks out and asks about our trip to Italy. I tell her everything concerning the help for Reach Charity, the money my grandma gave, and Sofia's wanting to have a fund-raising event at her villa.

Then Rachel jumps in, saying, "Aren't you forgetting something, Tara? Maybe the most important part."

"The juicy part was left for last," I say jokingly.

Jane looks at me with curiosity, so I tell the tale of meeting Lorenzo at my grandma's villa and everything that followed. Jane kisses me, saying it was about time.

"Oh my God. Why is everybody saying that? My angel, my mom, and now you," I say. "I wasn't ready, and the time wasn't right till now. Tell that to yourself Jane. Why do you keep bringing excuses?"

"It isn't the time now, and I haven't met the right guy yet," Jane replies.

The next morning after our coffee, we leave with Jane for the women's center. Rachel and I are excited to go back and see our friends. We walk with the center's director, Asha and Jane, to the women's education center for Reach Charity. It feels wonderful to see the efforts and donations of so many kind souls being used to assist people in need. The building is complete, and now we have to furnish the classrooms and purchase the equipment, and then it will be ready for use. Asha says she is proud of us for our commitment to helping others.

"But personally my life was enriched and meaningful the day I became conscious of my connection to the entire universe and felt it deep in my heart," I say. "When the fire of compassion was ignited in my soul, I decided to devote my time to service. I am extremely grateful for all the blessings in my life."

Rachel says, "Tara is right. It is an honor to be able to make a difference, even a little, and empower other people's lives."

Back at the center, Rachel and I want to invite them to lunch. Jane says, "We can't all leave and close the center, but I can call Mark's restaurant and ask him to deliver food for everybody."

It is a great idea, so we go to the dining room, set the table, and invite some of the young women who are there seeking help to eat with us. It ends up being one of the most enjoyable and memorable meals I have ever shared with friends.

In the evening, we go home together and see Tony waiting at the door to take Rachel out for dinner. Jane and I spend a relaxed and quiet evening. She asks me about Lorenzo and his humanitarian aid with other doctors, and wonders whether they have ever been to Tanzania. I explain their work but don't think they have been to Tanzania; maybe that would be next. Rachel comes home, and we go to bed, and I miss Lorenzo.

Every day we go to the center and help with a variety of cases. We are also furnishing the new education center and getting ready for the opening. I go with Jane to purchase the desks for the classrooms and also equipment and material needed for doing crafts. Everything is ready for accepting the young girls and women who would like to learn some skills for improving their lives.

I can't stop thinking about Atal and other girls and boys like her who are taken from their villages, terribly abused, and forced to do prostitution or hard work at homes or factories. We think there is no more slavery in the world, but this is the same and even worse because it mostly affects children and young women.

I pray for guidance from the universe for ways to help more. At night I see my angel telling me, "This is your mission, Tara, to travel and bring awareness to this dire issue facing humanity. You can build safe houses or healing centers for the victims of trafficking and help them, but this is a huge problem and requires the attention and efforts of all nations."

In the morning I share what my angel said with Rachel and Jane. "We have to focus on educating people about this matter. By describing the horrors that the trafficked children, young girls, and women go through, we can raise compassion and empathy in people's hearts."

One night Rachel is out with Tony, and Jane and I are enjoying our dinner. The doorbell rings; opening it, I see Lorenzo standing there. It is such an unexpected surprise that I just stand there, holding the door half open and staring at him. He waits a few moments and then gently pushes the door open and, holding me in his arms, lifts me up. I scream and start kissing him, saying, "What are you doing here?"

Poor Jane runs to see what is happening and, seeing us kissing, calmly says, "Oh, this must be Lorenzo." Jane is always calm, and I have never seen her lose her composure.

I lead him inside, saying, "Sorry, Jane, for screaming."

Jane welcomes him and brings another plate, inviting Lorenzo to eat with us. I say, "What are you doing in Arusha? And when did you arrive?"

"Seeing you, isn't that enough reason to travel across the world?" he says, laughing. "We arrived yesterday to Arusha with our doctors' group and went to the hospital. Then I contacted Tony and got Jane's address." That tricky Tony didn't tell me anything.

Jane opens a bottle of wine and asks about Lorenzo's work and how long he and his groups are staying in Arusha. When Tony and Rachel come home, I say, "Why didn't you tell me that Lorenzo was coming here?"

Tony hugs me. "Then what kind of a surprise would that be?"

Around midnight Lorenzo wants to leave, saying the next day he is going to call us, and Tony goes to drop him off at the hotel. Lorenzo calls around noon the next day and comes to the women's center. I show him around, and then we walk to the new educational center for Reach Charity. He wants to invite the other doctors in his group to visit the center and ask them to donate for hiring the teachers.

Back at the women's center, we share this idea with Rachel, Asha, and Jane. They all like and approve it, so we start planning for a casual informational lunch. Lorenzo has to go back to the hospital but invites us for dinner.

In the evening Tony picks him up from his hotel, and we all go to Mark's restaurant. Lorenzo is going to stay in Arusha, working at the hospital for two weeks, and then will go to Kenya with his group for the rest of the month, and from there to Somalia and back to Italy. At home Jane tells me she really likes Lorenzo and thinks Grandma Rita is right; we are a true match.

Reach's learning center is open, and we already have fifty girls and women of all ages who would like to improve the quality of their lives and every day take classes there. Rachel and I teach English and provide legal assistance, if needed. Educating women and girls is essential for the advancement of any society. When a mother is educated, she definitely will try to seek education for her children. This way the family, and consequently the entire community, will progress.

At night Lorenzo and I go out to dinner, and Rachel has plans with Tony. Sometimes we all go out with Jane or eat at home together. Lorenzo invites me to visit Kenya with him, saying he knows few people there who work in humanitarian organizations for different causes. I like the idea since we had a plan for a trip to Kenya, and it also gives me the opportunity to be alone with him. I discuss the idea with Rachel and Jane, asking for their opinions.

Rachel says, "This is a great opportunity to connect with some people who work there, and my angel said we should go to Kenya, and now the universe is providing the necessary resources."

Jane asks whether Lorenzo and I have ever been intimate, to which my answer is, no.

She laughs. "What are you waiting for, girl? This is the perfect time to share a hotel room with him."

"We have never been alone except going to restaurants, and I couldn't spend the night at his place in Italy."

"I am sure Grandma Rita would approve and be happy for you," Rachel says.

"Enough of that, you two. We are going for work, not for a honeymoon. That is just an added bonus," I say joyfully.

The next day Rachel asks Tony to join us on the trip to Kenya. In one week four of us are on our way there. We travel with the other doctors on their private bus. The young doctors from different nationalities have many tales of their travels to tell us. Before entering Kenya, we have to stop at the busy border for passport check, which takes about an hour, and then we are on the road again to Nairobi, the capital of Kenya. We arrive at the hotel after six hours of bus travel. Tony and Rachel go to their room, but for some strange reason, I feel nervous about sharing a room with Lorenzo.

Kenya is a country of many contrasts, from its landscape to its demographics and also to its social and economic state. It is one of the most wildlife-rich countries in Africa, with many national parks. Every year a large number of tourists from all around the world visit Kenya. A great inequality exists in Kenya, and many people live below poverty line and don't have access to health care or education. Nairobi, also known as "Green City in the Sun," is a large, crowded, and multiethnic city; people from all cultures and backgrounds blend together.

We walk to a restaurant near the hotel, which the polite guy at the reception has recommended. The food is delicious, and we have such a great, fun time that I try to stretch by asking for more dessert and wine, trying to avoid returning to our room. Noticing my hesitation, Rachel kicks me under the table, saying, "We are tired from the long drive. Let's go back to our room."

I am a little nervous, but Lorenzo is so gentle and understanding that he puts me at ease, and we make passionate love for hours and fall sleep in each other's arms. In the morning we join Rachel and Tony for breakfast. Lorenzo calls one of his friends, the director of an organization working to empower girls and women in Kenya, and asks if she can meet with us, saying we might want to collaborate with them. He and the other doctors will work at a medical clinic located near the slums, where low-income families live. We catch a taxi and go to our appointment with Lorenzo's friend.

Raziya, a kind woman in her sixties, greets us warmly and takes us to her office. I ask about their work and if we can help in anyway. She tells us gender inequality is a big problem in Kenya, though government and different organizations are working on behalf of girls and women, trying to change that. But the problem is vast and needs effort and funds. She continues, saying that in low-income areas of Nairobi and other cities of Kenya, girls have a disadvantage in education and health care. Because of poverty, they are forced to early marriage and unwanted sexual activity.

"We have many teenage pregnancy and HIV cases, even in very young girls," she says. "Girls are subjected to domestic violence from their fathers, brothers, or much older husbands. In our organization, we want to stop violence against young girls and women by providing education for them and their parents. We dedicate our efforts and resources to raise awareness on the issue of sexual violence and girls trafficking for sexual exploitation. We also provide health care for low-income families."

I say we can talk to our members and provide some funds and that my passion is clearly on eradicating sexual exploitation. Girls and women are divine souls like everyone else in the world, not objects to be sold, traded, and used for pleasure against their wills. We leave Raziya, thanking her for meeting with us.

Rachel, Tony, and I do some sight-seeing in the streets of Nairobi and do some souvenir shopping at the open-air Maasai Market. There are all kinds of nicknacks in these markets, and wood-carvings, many hand-made in Kenya by local artisans. It is fun to haggle for finding the best deal.

Lorenzo is working till late evening at the clinic and then will join us at the hotel to go out for dinner. We stop at a café for some tea and a snack, and then we walk to the hotel, where we go to our rooms.

In our room, seeing Lorenzo's pants and shirts hanging in the closet gives me a warm and homey feeling. I have never felt as loved as the way he treats and adores me. I love Lorenzo and feel happy and complete with him. I'm grateful to the universe for bringing him into my life.

I sit for a long meditation and see my soul flying freely with joy. I see the face of God with extreme love for humanity and all beings, including animals, plants, and everything else in the world. I come back when Lorenzo enters the room, hugging me and saying how much he has missed me.

We join Rachel and Tony at the hotel lobby and walk out to go to a restaurant. We grab a cab and go to the center, where there are many places to eat. We choose a restaurant that says European and African food. The food is delicious, the wine is great, and we are all happy and content; everything is perfect. The next day after breakfast Lorenzo goes back to the clinic, and we ask the hotel to arrange a tour of the Nairobi National Park for us.

The park is only seven kilometers from the center of Nairobi City with its skyscrapers and modern buildings. It is a safe haven for wildlife and also a rhino sanctuary. More than fifty of these critically endangered animals due to cruel poaching are protected in the sanctuary. We see some lions walking proudly, also buffalo, cheetahs, zebras, giraffes, gazelles, and ostriches. Seeing these beautiful creatures, I am in awe and appreciate all God's blessings even more.

After the tour, we thank our tour guide and go back to the hotel. Lorenzo tells us we are going to dinner with all the doctors in the group. We all meet at the hotel lobby and decide to walk to a restaurant close to the hotel. There are a few restaurants, such as Italian, French, seafood, and some others. We choose the one that serves African and Italian.

The servers put few tables together to accommodate our large group. I sit next to Paul, a young cardiologist from France who travels every year with Lorenzo and the rest of the group to different countries. He comes from a family of doctors; his parents and grandparents all work in France half of the year and travel, seeing patients for free the rest of the year. He says his grandfather is almost ninety years old but looks like he's in his sixties; he is energetic with great stamina, still traveling and working long hours.

"People who have love and compassion for all in their heart, helping others, stay young and active and have an ageless quality, even in their eighties, nineties, or more," Paul says. "But people with negative attitudes and self-pity look old and tired, even if they are thirty years old."

"I hope we can be active and serve when we are more than eighty or ninety years old," I reply.

We order wine and a few different dishes to share. Everyone tells stories from his or her native town and the countries he or she has visited. We have a fantastic dinner, but it's now midnight, and the doctors have to work the next day. They want to close the restaurant, so Lorenzo says, "Let's leave before they throw us out."

Lorenzo and I make passionate love till almost morning, and after a few short hours of sleep, we join Rachel and Tony for breakfast. There are two more days left in our Kenya trip, and Lorenzo has to work. But we want to visit Raziya and confirm our commitment to help educating and empowering adolescent girls and young women in Kenya.

We are back in Arusha and happy to be with Jane and see Asha. But I am also sad since Lorenzo has to leave for Italy soon. Rachel and I go to Reach's educational center for visiting and talking to the young girls and women, asking about their progress. They are all excited and hopeful, looking forward to a better life.

I make an inquiry about the absence of a very smart, young girl who had advanced and was thriving. One of the teachers tells us her abusive husband found out she was seeking education and beat her up so badly that the neighbors had to interfere and take her to the hospital. I was exuberant, seeing the girls happy, but now this awful news is disconcerting and disturbing.

We rush to the hospital and see her purple, black, and swollen face; both Rachel and I have tears in our eyes. Her legs are broken and in braces, and her eyes are closed to a narrow line. But hearing our voices, she tries to form a faded smile on her injured lips.

I hold her hand, trying to say some comforting words. But honestly, I am just furious and enraged at this injustice, and words fall short in expressing it. Rachel and I stay at her bedside for most of the day and leave in the evening, promising to visit her again. Back at the center, I ask Asha if they have taken any action against her husband. She says that the center's attorney had talked to him, but the wife Zoya, doesn't want to file a complaint.

At home I discuss with Jane and Rachel the ways we can help and seek justice for her. In bed I pray to my angel, asking how we can protect and guaranty her safety.

In my deep sleep, I see my angel, with a sad expression on her bright face, saying, "You are all heavenly spirits and one with God, each other, and everything in the world. You should feel this connection in your heart and soul, stopping to hurt one another. The only way to heal the humanity, your beautiful mother earth, and the world is to have compassion and love for everyone and everything in your heart, and to be of service and a source of comfort to each-other whenever and wherever you can. Love is the necessity for survival of the universe. Love yourself, God, and one-another. Love is like an adhesive that keeps everything together, living and dancing in harmony."

In the morning I tell Jane and Rachel what my angel said with a renewed commitment in my heart. Jane has to go to work, but Rachel and I walk to the hospital. Zoya is happy to see us, but in response to our inquiry about her husband's violent actions, she says, "We have a son together, and he is a good father, although a cruel husband to me, but I forgive him and don't want him to be in prison. Please talk to my husband and make him understand that education is good and helps our family. I can work and make money and provide a better life for our son."

Rachel and I promise to do whatever is possible to convince her husband and make sure something like this doesn't happen anymore.

We go back to the center and tell Asha we want to have a heart-to-heart conversation with Zoya's husband. She agrees to take us to their house. He is a man in his fifties, and Zoya is just nineteen, but we respect her wishes and try to make him comprehend the importance of education.

Asha says, "If it was up to me, you would be in prison now, but Zoya has graciously forgiven you. Try not to betray her trust."

As we are talking, an adorable three-year-old boy runs to his father's arms with a big smile on his face. Seeing their son, I understand Zoya's choice to stay with his husband. Thus, I start explaining the benefits of going to school and learning. After an hour of discussion, I finally feel a spark of light softening his heart and remorse for what he had done. He promises us to never raise his hand at Zoya again and to support her decisions.

Part 5

THE CONCLUSION OF OUR FIRST JOURNEY

Rachel and I are excited to celebrate the one-year anniversary of our adventurous journey of self-discovery, which has brought us so much blessings. We invite all our friends, Asha, and the teachers from Reach's educational center to Mark's restaurant for lunch.

We talk about our story and how it all started. I say, "Less than a year ago, Rachel and I started a journey to discover our purpose and true passion in life. We both had good jobs and earned a fair amount of money, thus leaving all that was scary. To tell you the truth,

I was nervous and unsure about quitting my job against my boss's and my mom's advice. And Rachel was taking the journey because of me. But on the airplane on our way to Tanzania, I made a pledge to let go of the past hurts and go forward wholeheartedly, not being frightened by the size of the task. With God's grace, all the doors opened up to us, and resources were provided. Our dear, generous Jane accommodated Rachel and me in her beautiful house. You know the rest of the story."

"Not only did we discover our purpose and true passion in life, but we found much more. In doing our work, I felt my oneness with God and the entire universe. We met extraordinary people like you who so humbly are serving others without expecting any rewards. I speak for Rachel, too, saying how grateful we are for your friendship and kindness. Since the beginning of this journey, our lives have been enriched with an abundance of blessings. I know now that when the universe calls, we should answer and show up, being prepared to do the task. As my angel said, we wish to expand our Reach and extend our helping hand to more places and countries. We are all one with God, one another, and the entire universe; and we must care and help in any way possible. But each of us has a unique purpose that has to be fulfilled and lived. This way we can shine our light and accomplish extraordinary endeavors."

"Tara talked a lot, and we want to start our lunch," Rachel says. "Therefore, I say double everything she said. In a few days, we are flying to New York but will be back to Arusha and then to Nepal and after that wherever else God directs us to go."

Soon we are back in New York and sitting around the dinner table at my mom's place with her boyfriend and our families. My mom raises her glass of wine and says, "Tara and Rachel, I admire your tenacity for following your dreams and making a difference in the world. And thanks for encouraging me to take meditation and explaining how changing my mind changes my life."

Rachel and I thank our family for their love and support, and then I say, "We had a dream and a spark of inspiration that Rachel and I followed. We took the first step with faith, and every day did our part and left the details to the universe without interfering or getting in the way. And as you know, by the grace of God the universe came through in a big way and provided all the necessary resources. We really didn't put much effort into it or toil over it. In fact, Rachel and I enjoyed every moment of it, and our lives have improved, and as the result, we are happier than we ever have been. We just moved out of our comfort zone, took the first step, and every day did our best.

"As the ancient Chinese philosopher Lao Tzu says, 'The journey of a thousand miles begins with one step.' When we are aligned with our purpose, doing what we love, an inexhaustible source of energy flows through us by heaven."

Rachel and I meet with the other members of Reach charity to discuss our future projects. And we also decide on other countries we would like to expand our help to. Then I say, "We have to strive every day to improve and elevate ourselves, and to break all the barriers of self-imposed limitation. And we should help and empower others. We each have a purpose in life that we have to fulfill and play our part. But at the same time, we have to get out of our ego-self and coordinate our efforts collectively for the well-being of everyone and everything in the universe."

"I understand that not everyone can quit their jobs and leave their families to travel the world and help others. But there is always plenty to do in our own city or even our neighborhood, if we are willing to look and undertake the task. Sometimes all we have to do is just be kind and respect one-another."

Then I continue, "In my opinion, if you all agree, we should expand our Reach to many more countries to help and raise awareness about human trafficking and sex exploitation. Thus, the road ahead is long, and we have much more to do. But with love, compassion, and determination, it could all be done joyfully. I love this quote by Dalai Lama. 'Human potential is the same for all. If you have willpower, then you can change anything.'"

Rachel and I talk and decide to stay in New York for some time and start our own law firm. We can work to earn some money and then start our travels again, while sustaining our current projects. But first we have a trip to Italy and England.

We are at the airport again, but this time Rachel and I go to different destinations. Rachel is going to England to be with Tony, who is visiting his parents. My mom, Tom, and I are going to Italy, since she wants to introduce her boyfriend to Grandma Rita, and I will spend some delicious time with Lorenzo.

Till we meet again, I would like to leave you with this quote from Albert Einstein.

"A human being is a part of the whole called by us the universe, a part limited in time and space. We experience ourselves, our thoughts and feelings as something separated from the rest, a kind of optical delusion of our consciousness. This delusion is a kind of prison for us, restricting us to our personal desires and to affection for a few persons nearest to us. Our task must be to free ourselves from this self-imposed prison by widening our circle of compassion to embrace all living creatures and the whole of nature in its beauty."

Reach, reach out, and extent your
arms with love and compassion.

Reach, reach out, and touch someone's
life with kindness and generosity.

Reach, reach out, and touch the stars
and beyond with God's love. (Author)

About the Author

Grace is a Meditation and Self-improvement coach. She has lived in Europe for many year, and now lives in the US. Grace loves traveling and doing humanitarian works.

The proceeds of this book is donated by the author to the Children Charity www.momsagainstpoverty.org.

Printed in the United States
By Bookmasters